Knowing
And
Experiencing
God

God will never be real to you until you have a healthy visual

concept of Him as He really is

i

Knowing
And
Experiencing
God

God will never be real to you until you have a healthy visual

concept of Him as He really is

Arthur S. Meintjes

KNOWING AND EXPERIENCING GOD

God will never be real to you until you have a healthy visual concept of Him as He really is.

This book was adapted from an eight part audio series by Arthur Meintjes entitled "Knowing and Experiencing God".

Transcriber and Executive Editor: Jay Randolph
Assistant Editor/Proofreader: Les Raley
Favor Communications International
PO Box 19636 Denver, CO 80219

Published in South Africa 2005 & 2007 by
Kingdom Life Ministries Publications
PO Box 13674 Middelburg Mpumalanga
1050 South Africa

Printed in USA 2010 by
Kingdom Life Ministries Publications
3802 Galileo Dr #C
Fort Collins, CO 80528

Printed by: Corporate Colours, Bedfordview South Africa

Additional Editing by: Cathy Meintjes

Cover Design by: Caleb Miller

Acknowledgements

nowing and experiencing God would never have been written, and printed without the support and encouragement of a multitude of wonderful people, of which my family are first and foremost. I am so grateful to my wife Cathy. You have been my biggest supporter, encourager and sometimes critic but always loving, caring and absolutely sensitive of my feelings. You have been my best friend, advisor and thank the Lord a tender lover. I love you with all my heart. To my daughters Cheri-Anne and Gabby, and my son AJ, thanks for putting up with me working long hours and many of them away from home. You are all bright shining stars who brighten my sometimes-lonely nights.

Thanks to my dear friends Darryl Hendricks, and Grant Wishart without whom the printing of this book would still only be a dream. Thanks guys for your wisdom, and also your belief in this project and me, even when it sometimes looked like it was not going to happen.

A special thanks to all our supporters around the world who all from time to time contributed in various ways to this book, without you there would have been no reason to write this book. To Jay Randall for helping to make this book a reality through your editing skills. To my good friend Pastor Allen Speegle, and his awesome congregation in Eustis, FL, and to Andrew Wommack for your consistent encouragement to use and believe in the gifts of God in me.

I want to give a special thanks to a friend and someone whom I greatly value, Dr James B. Richards. So much of this book is a direct result of your influence through your books, teaching and practical modeling of the Gospel of Grace and Peace. I am eternally grateful.

Above all I give heart felt thanks to my Abba Father God, whose love, mercy and grace has transformed my life through the Lord Jesus Christ. All glory, honor and praise be to you for ever and ever.

INDEX   Page

Introduction

Some very important and foundational truths are consistently neglected in the spiritual lives of many Christians today. Without these proper foundations, believers cannot really go on to "stronger meat" and "deeper intimacy." I have tested this observation wherever I go, and have seen it proven true again and again throughout the years, both in my traveling ministry and pastoral experience. Wherever I have ministered God's Word, I have found that many believers are not really relating to God day by day based upon New Testament realities.

In addressing believers in Hebrews 5:12-13 Paul says: *"For though by this time you ought to be teachers, you need someone to teach you again the first principles of the oracles of God; and you have come to need milk and not solid food. For everyone who partakes only of milk is unskilled in the word of righteousness, for he is a babe."* NKJV

The essence of what He said was, "I could not speak to you as grown men and women of God who are mature because your foundations were never solidly laid." For many, many years of my Christian life and ministry that was who I was! I was spiritually stuck and could not go on with God because I had a faulty foundation and did not even know it.

Believe me, lack of information was not the problem! My head swam with much Christian knowledge from attending Bible school and studying concordances, dictionaries, and commentaries. However, this multitude of information that I had accumulated from the years spent in preparation for, and later being involved in, fulltime ministry did not adequately address my real need. Finally, I came to a point in my life when I realized that I could not really go on with God because solid foundations had never been properly laid in my own heart.

As I came to this pivotal place in my life and ministry, the Lord began to reveal to me that I am now living in the New Testament, and not the Old. God did not change, but the basis of my daily relationship to Him did. The fundamental difference lies in the fact that I am no longer trusting in my own performance, but rather in Christ's performance, concerning every aspect of my life of faith. God Himself stepped out of the types and shadows of the Old Testament to fully reveal Himself in the New Testament through His Son.

I wrote this book because I want you also to be able to go on with God. My goal is to lay within your heart a sure foundation for knowing and experiencing Him. The revelation of the Father heart of God completely, powerfully, and permanently transformed my personal life and worldwide ministry. Today, this message of

Introduction

His goodness and love burns as a white-hot fire in my bones and remains centered in the heart of all I preach and teach.

Dear friend, get ready—Your Heavenly Father has some treasures He wants to bless you with through these revelation packed pages. You are about to encounter God in ways you have never experienced before! Please do not let some old sacred cows of religious thinking hold you back from a more intimate relationship with Him. I can assure you, He is not worth missing out on for anything. Go ahead, taste and see for yourself that the Lord is good!

One

Behold His Glory

Over the past two or three decades, the Body of Christ around the world has been blessed by an abundance of good and readily available Bible teaching. Much quality knowledge has been put out for believers to receive into their lives. For the most part, this has been a good thing. However, this vast amount of knowledge has also contributed to some problems. I Corinthians 8:1 tells us that knowledge puffs us up, but love builds us up. Many believers who have taken in all that spiritual knowledge over the years begin to give in to a subtle form of pride. When they are around other Christians who do not have the "right" answers, they judge them, saying in their hearts, "Until you have the doctrines down pat like I do, you will remain a lesser Christian than me!" They have forgotten that the believer's life is not just about acquiring large amounts of "correct" information.

Standing Before Him

When you stand before God one day, He will not quiz you over the finer points of Bible trivia. The one question you must answer affirmatively is, "Do you know Jesus Christ as your Lord and Saviour?" You qualify if your answer is, "Yes!" He will not thoroughly cross-examine you to see if you had all of the current doctrines down pat. No, He will say, "Come on in!" It is all about knowing Him!

When you know Jesus Christ, you are assured of your salvation. You have confidence before God the Father. Personally, I did not have much confidence before Him for most of my Christian life. Many, many Christians suffer from this lack of confidence for the same reason I did: I never felt I performed to the level I thought would bring me the confidence I needed to stand before Him. Is that you today? Are you trying to gain your confidence before God through achieving an elusive level of performance in your Christian life? Were you once "saved by grace," but today find yourself functionally trying to earn your "sanctification" and ability to approach God through all of your good "Christian" works? If so, I have good news for you!

The Holy Spirit inspired and guided a man named Paul to write two-thirds of the New Testament. God used this man mightily to record the revelation of the goodness, love and grace of God. Considering Paul's life, he sure knew what he was talking about! God transformed this murderous religious fanatic into the man who was willing to gladly endure tremendous amounts of suffering for his proclamation of the Gospel. He lived to proclaim the awesome love of God that had been revealed to Him through Christ Jesus to as many people as he could in his lifetime. Today, we praise God that He used Paul to do some writing while Paul was in prison. Under the inspiration of the Holy Spirit Himself, Paul recorded his letters to various churches, including this one to the Ephesians that we are about to look at.

In Paul's letters, whenever you read the phrase, "I always pray this for you," I recommend that you pay special attention to what the Holy Spirit had him write next. Every time I have run across this phrase, I have discovered an awesome foundational truth for my Christian life today. Paul knew that if these foundational truths were not established in the hearts of believers, they would not be able to go on with God. I am someone who wants to go on with God. I can tell that you are too because you are reading this book! You have begun this journey because you desire to live a more fulfilled Christian life than you ever have before. Be encouraged! God is even more excited about this than you are!

Wisdom and Revelation

Therefore I also, after I heard of your faith in the Lord Jesus and your love for all the saints, do not cease to give thanks for you, making mention of you in my prayers: that the God of our Lord Jesus Christ, the Father of glory, may give to you the spirit of wisdom and revelation in the knowledge of Him, the eyes of your understanding being enlightened; that you may know what is the hope of His calling, what are the riches of the glory of His inheritance in the saints, and what is the exceeding greatness of His power toward us who believe, according to the working of His mighty power which He worked in Christ when He raised Him from the dead and seated Him at His right hand in the heavenly places, far above all principality and power and might and dominion, and every name that is named, not only in this age but also in that which is to come. (Ephesians 1:15-21) NKJV

"(I) do not cease to give thanks for you, making mention of you in my prayers" (Ephesians 1:16). Paul wrote to these believers saying that he talked about them in his prayers. I learned this lesson many years ago. It is wise not to talk about other people unless you are genuinely in prayer for them. Avoid the temptation to turn a time of prayer into a gossip session!

"That the God of our Lord Jesus Christ, the Father of glory…" (Ephesians 1:17). God is the Father of glory! "Glory" means "fullness." One of the understandings we get from the definition of the word "glory" in the Bible speaks of "the view and opinion of God which is reality." God's view and opinion is the only true reality there is. Did you know that God has an opinion about you? Yes, He sure does! If you will find out what His view and opinion about you is, everybody else's view and opinion, including your own, will not matter so much to you any more.

I (Paul) pray that He *"…may give unto you the spirit of wisdom and revelation in the knowledge of him"* (Ephesians 1:17). Paul constantly prayed this for all of the believers he carried on his heart. He interceded that they may have insight into the mysteries and secrets of the deep intimate knowledge of Him (God). He prayed this for

7

an important reason: Paul wanted them to receive a revelation of who God is. *"The eyes of your understanding being enlightened" (18).* He wanted the very eyes of their hearts to be flooded with divine light or truth!

I have noticed that much of the "knowledge" floating around in many Christian circles today does not seem to fill believers with light, life and truth. What is wrong with such "revelation"? Well, we need to discern whether the "knowledge" being presented to us is religion, or a true revelation of God's nature and character. What does it produce in our lives? What is the fruit of it? Is it fear or is it love?

An Angry God?

Religion has always presented God as an angry God who needs to be appeased. Have you ever been exposed to such preaching and teaching? Perhaps you have not heard it expressed in those exact words, but the messages and attitudes have painted the same mental picture. Many Christians view God as an angry God who will not be friendly or gracious toward them until they can do what it takes to appease Him. Have you ever felt the need to "do what it takes?" As a mere religious system, Christianity has given the world this awful picture of an "angry God."

I know, because I believed this way for most of my Christian life! It was not until recent years that I have been able to find the words to explain the way I felt. It seemed to me that God just tolerated me because He had to. Even though I had received the Lord Jesus Christ as my personal Lord and Savior, I did not feel accepted by God. From my perspective, God was forced to

8

accept me because of the shed blood of Jesus, but He sure did not like me! I believed He felt obligated to receive me just because I had received His Son.

Why did I feel this way? In my heart, I knew that I could not really live up to the way the church and other Christians told me I should live. The standards of morality and spirituality that were portrayed to me as "normal and required daily living" were way out of my reach. Since I could not attain to them, I assumed that God just tolerated me because He had to. God did not really like me. Have you ever felt this way? Can you relate to what I am saying?

You can never really get to the place where your heart can be filled with the light Ephesians 1:17-18 talks about until you begin to see the true Father heart of God. "Light" and "life" in the Bible are often synonymous. When your heart is full of His light, you will also be full of His life.

His Child

To finish the rest of verse 18, "*...that you may know what is the hope of His calling, what are the riches of the glory of His inheritance in the saints*" If you do not know God for who He really is, you will not be able to understand the hope to which He has called you. If you do not have an intimate revelation of who He really is, you will be unable to grasp this hope, the hope of being a child of God.

1 John 3:1-2 declares, "*Behold, what manner of love the Father hath bestowed upon us, that we should be called the sons of God: therefore the*

world knoweth us not, because it knew him not. Beloved, now are we the sons of God, and it doth not yet appear what we shall be: but we know that, when he shall appear, we shall be like him; for we shall see him as he is."

"Behold" means "look!" It is an old English word that was used to grab your attention. What does verse 1 tell you to look at? The love of the Father. Whose love? The Father's Love! Firstly, you must put your full attention on your Father's awesome love for you!

"Beloved, now are we the sons of God." When? Now! You are a child of God. Let that sink in a little bit…a child of God. *"…and it doth not yet appear what we shall be: but we know that, when he shall appear, we shall be like him; for we shall see him as he is."* I used to preach this section of scripture solely from the perspective of the Second Coming of Christ. I would tell people that we would be transformed into His likeness when He appears in the sky. Although this interpretation could be true, it is not complete. The Lord has since shown me another important insight from this passage.

The Family Likeness

I want you to read the second half of verse 2 again. *"…but we know that, when he shall appear, we shall be like him; for we shall see him as he is."* The powerful insight He revealed to me from this scripture is this: As God reveals Himself to us out of the Word, our view of Him is affected and in effect changed. Then, when we start to see God for who He really is, we will find out that we are already just like Him.

10

Can you see it? Go ahead and reread that last statement again, slowly. Let each word's meaning sink in to your understanding until you can see it. As God reveals Himself to us out of the Word, our view of Him is affected. Then, when we start to see God for who He really is, we will find out that we are just like Him.

Why do so many believers lead such weak Christian lives? Why do they fail so often and so badly? I believe the major reason is that they are not looking with the eyes of their heart at the true appearance of God our Father. The Bible is very clear in communicating the fact that Jesus Christ came and gave us the full expression of who God is. He held nothing back from us. In Jesus, we see the fullness of our Father!

This scripture says that when He appears to us, we shall be like Him. Why? When you and I accurately see Him, in whose nature and image we have been made new through rebirth, we will be like Him from that moment on. That moment can be as soon as you see Him. It does not have to be the split second you cross over into eternity one day in the future. It can be now, while you are living out your life here on earth! The bottom line is seeing Him the way He is. Then, you will be like Him. It is a basic principle of life as a human being. You and I become like the "God" we look to, love, and serve. This is just how we are designed!

Just like a coin, this truth has a tails side as well. If you do not see God for who He really is, you will still be transformed into the image of the "God" you see. Allow me to illustrate this for you. Have you ever met a Christian that is mean, angry and hard to

11

please? I certainly have. I used to be one of them. In fact, I was probably one of the meanest of them all! Do you know why many Christians are so mean? Simply put, it is this very principle in action. The "God" they know and serve is a mean "God," so they reflect the likeness of the "God" they see and serve. 1 John 3:2 very clearly says, that if you can see Him as He is, then you can be transformed into His likeness.

True Transformation

I want to be changed into His likeness, not the likeness of some distorted view of who I think He is, or who religion says He is. I desire change for the things in my life that need to change. Do you? I always knew that I needed to change, but could never figure out how to actually do it. I wanted to change, but had no hope of truly being transformed. Believe me, I tried! I was stuck until the Lord revealed this truth of seeing Him accurately. I recognized that I needed to see Him for who He really is and not the distortion of who I thought He was that I had previously been seeing.

2 Corinthians 3:17-18 also illuminates this powerful truth. *"Now the Lord is that Spirit: and where the Spirit of the Lord is, there is liberty. But we all, with open face beholding as in a glass the glory of the Lord, are changed into the same image from glory to glory, even as by the Spirit of the Lord."* Understanding the word "glory" is the key to comprehending this passage. As we have already seen, the word "glory" is talking about God's fullness, splendor and goodness. It is also talking about "God's view and opinion, which is reality." Notice that this verse says that you and I are seeing God's glory with an unveiled face. You are a New Covenant believer beholding

as in a mirror (God's Word) the glory of God. (James 1:22-25). The Old Covenant veil guarding and shrouding the entrance to the Holy of Holies has been torn away and laid aside since the cross. As you behold (look at) His glory, you are changed into the same image from glory to glory. As you see His view and opinion, which is reality, His splendor and His goodness, you are transformed, or changed into His likeness.

How does true and lasting change come into your life? Does this permanent kind of change occur through putting forth effort? Each New Year, many people make resolutions in an attempt to bring the needed change into their lives. They are sick and tired of their lives. New Year's Day comes along and they decide to do something about it. They even go so far as to listen to motivational speakers who give them strategies for setting and pursuing their goals. All they have to do is put some action to them, right? All you have to do is become a man or woman who can commit and follow through. Have you ever done this?

These things do work to a certain extent. You can change your behavior, but it does not mean that your heart has been changed. These efforts may be working externally, but this does not mean that you are truly changing internally. Most of the time you are just imposing an outward form upon yourself that works for as long as you have the willpower to maintain it. Then, when the willpower gives out, your old self comes back out again because your heart was not changed. This is when you normally become disappointed and get depressed. Some people find themselves so far down that they have to go to the doctor to get antidepressants.

13

True effortless transformation and change occurs from the inside out! The scripture says that we are transformed by beholding. Everything has to do with who or what it is that you are continually looking at. Let me ask you this question. As a Christian, have you ever bought an idol made of wood, metal, or clay and brought it home to worship? No! Well I hope not! Why not? Christians do not worship idols! We do not purchase them. We do not bring them into our homes. Certainly, we are not going to light candles and sacrifice foods to them like those who worship idols do. We follow Jesus, not idols!

Did you know that the Bible word for "idol" literally just means "an image". An image is an idol. As a Christian, when you have a wrong image of who God is, you may as well just worship an idol! I can see you cringing in your seat. None of us want that. We all want to be able to see God for who He really is!

My Prayer

Most Christians have no trouble recognizing the fact that God is all-powerful, all present, and all knowing. I start to lose people when I begin to discuss with them the Father heart of God. Many believers have little or no concept of knowing God as their Father. They may call Him by the title "Father" because Jesus taught them to do so in the Bible, but they actually relate to Him as "God Almighty" an angry God who needs constant appeasing. They pray the prayer Jesus taught them saying, "Our Father..." but in their hearts and lives they have never truly known Him in such a loving and intimate way.

Personally, I used to be one of those Christians. I could mouth the words, "Father" at times, but I really related to Him from my heart as "God Almighty" an angry God who needs constant appeasing I usually felt like He was angry with me. I was driven to do my best to keep Him happy. As long as my good works outweighed my bad works—so I thought—God would be happy with me.

As Paul prayed for the believers, I am praying for you. I am asking Him to give you a spirit of wisdom and revelation in the knowledge of who He really is. May the eyes of your heart be enlightened with understanding so that you can experience more and more of His goodness and love!

Two

Taste and See!

O
ne of the most important things for you to understand as you begin this journey to knowing and experiencing God is to know that God is a good God. Yes, God is a good God! Psalm 34:8 proclaims, *"O taste and see that the Lord is good: blessed is the man that trusteth in him."* David wrote, "...taste and see." Now what is taste? Taste is an experience. When you taste, you are experiencing something.

What you believe affects your emotions. If what you "believe" does not affect your emotions, then you have not truly believed! You say, "But Arthur, I am not moved by emotions. I am moved by faith!" True faith will produce emotions. If the emotions you are currently experiencing contradict the Word of God, then start believing the Word and watch your emotions change. The principle holds true that what you truly believe in your heart affects your emotions.

Taste and See!

Assured of His Goodness

The emotions you currently have toward God reveal what you really believe to be true right now concerning your relationship with Him. How you feel about God shows what you really believe about Him. Take a moment right now to stop and reflect on the recent emotions you have been experiencing about God. What does this tell you about what you really believe?

I want you to be able to experience God's goodness! I want you to taste and see that God is good. Yes God is good! In the original language of Psalm 34:8, the word "is" used here means "is equal to" Therefore, God is equal to good and good is equal to God. God is equal to love and love is equal to God! (1 John 4:16)

While traveling in the USA, I met a South African lady in Pennsylvania who was a nervous wreck and emotionally disturbed When I first started ministering to her, she said, "Hang on, Arthur! You just cannot go overboard with this 'God is love and goodness' stuff! You need to balance this out!" Now my question is this, how do you balance "God is equal to good" out? What counterbalance is there for "God is equal to love?" This is the balance because God is good and God is love! Hallelujah!

God wants you to get this truth firmly established in your heart. His desire is that you be <u>fully assured</u> of the fact that He is good. He wants your heart to be <u>fully persuaded</u> of the truth that He is good all the time. As a Christian, you will not be able to live an emotionally stable life until you honestly believe these truths. You just cannot do it!

17

David

God is a good God! If anybody mentioned in the Bible would know this, it would be David. It took me a while before I could see this in David's life. I had misconceptions about him because of the few times I attended Sunday School as a kid. To me David was always portrayed as such a wonderful man of faith. Don't get me wrong he was a great man. He was a man of faith, but the mental picture I had of him was of a man who never made any mistakes. I thought he always had it together. After all, he was a man after God's own heart, right?

Once I grew up and studied David's life for myself, I realized that he had made some major blunders! Perhaps his most glaring mistake was the whole sin fiasco with another man's wife. It happened at a time when David should have been down on the battlefield with his men. Instead, he was hanging back at the palace enjoying a warm summer's night on his roof. All of a sudden, he saw a UFO, an Unidentified Female Object, a beautiful young lady taking a bath!

David probably had his binoculars out like those guys in New York City. Almost every time I have been there, I have stayed with people who live in high-rise buildings. One time, the couple that hosted me lived in a penthouse on the 35th floor. It was a beautiful place! Upon my arrival, I walked in and saw this fellow's telescope there in the living room. So I naively asked him, "Do you look at the stars from here?"

He looked at me funny and replied, "No!! That is not what those things are used for here!" Apparently, these big city people use them to check out other people.

Anyway, King David saw this beautiful woman. The Bible tells us that she was drop dead gorgeous! He looked at her and must have said to himself, "I have got to have her! I am the king." Remember, this is David talking—the man after God's own heart. When I first saw this in the Word, I thought, "Lord, if there is room for David, there must be a place in heaven for me!"

After God's Own Heart

Of course, David went on to commit the adultery he had imagined in his heart. However, he did not stop sinning there. He added deception and murder to it after learning that Bathsheba got pregnant from their time together. He had this woman's rightful husband executed at the battlefront when he refused to lay with her on a short vacation. According to the law of God, David brought himself under a threefold death sentence. This is the same man who instructed us to "taste and see that God is good."

I believe that David was a man after God's own heart not because he always did the right thing but because he always chose to seek God as a good God no matter what his circumstances were. It did not matter that he was guilty of the vile sins of adultery, deception, and murder. This just shows that David was capable of being as wicked as anybody else. However, he trusted God to have mercy and be good to him. Looking upon that response, God declared, "Now that is a man after My own heart. He trusts Me to be good to him even in the midst of his failures!" God is impressed with people who will see and trust Him for who He really is, no matter what is happening in their lives.

The revelation of God's goodness permeates the pages of the Bible from beginning to end! In the New Covenant, we see the Person of Jesus Christ giving a full display of God's goodness for the world to see. Yet, in the Old Covenant, there are some extremely valuable glimpses of God's goodness as well. Even though He is only revealed in part, it is well worth our while to consider His goodness as revealed in the Old Testament. My goal throughout this book is to build a deep awareness of His goodness in your heart using the pages of scripture. You, too, will then be able to taste and see for yourself!

Three

Rest In His Goodness

N ow Moses was tending the flock of Jethro, his father-in-law, the priest of Midian, and he led the flock to the far side of the desert and came to Horeb, the mountain of God. There the angel of the LORD appeared to him in flames of fire from within a bush. Moses saw that though the bush was on fire it did not burn up. So Moses thought, "I will go over and see this strange sight--why the bush does not burn up." When the LORD saw that he had gone over to look, God called to him from within the bush, "Moses! Moses!" And Moses said, "Here I am."   (Exodus 3:1-4) NIV

By studying God's Word for myself, the Lord has shown me the faultiness of many of the opinions I used to hold. I discovered that many of the widely held Christian assumptions that I had bought into were not even related to reality as presented in the

Bible. Yet, these opinions actively influenced the way I read the scriptures.

For instance, I used to always assume that Moses knew God. Wherever I saw the name "Moses," I automatically thought that it was talking about a man who knew God well. After all, he is the figurehead of the Old Testament law! However, after I more fully understood this passage in Exodus, I realized that Moses really did not even have a clue as to who God really was. Please stay with me as we look more deeply into this matter together.

Moses initially met God at the burning bush as the Consuming Fire (Exodus 3:2, Hebrews 12:29). The bush burned, but was not consumed. It was a wonderful miracle that got his attention. The voice of God spoke to him saying, "Take off your shoes for this is holy ground. You have found grace in My sight. I am going to use you!" Wow! What an experience this must have been. This is the very first time Moses had ever spoken with God. He had no idea who God was. Remember, Moses had not been educated as a Hebrew child, but as a wealthy royal Egyptian.

Who Are You?

Then Moses said to the LORD, "See, You say to me, 'Bring up this people.' But You have not let me know whom You will send with me. Yet You have said, 'I know you by name, and you have also found grace in My sight.' Now therefore, I pray, if I have found grace in Your sight, show me now Your way, that I may know You and that I may find grace in Your sight. And consider that this nation is Your people."(Exodus 33:12-13) NKJV

Then, the Lord led Moses through the deliverance of the Israelites from Egypt. They passed through the Red Sea. There was provision of food, water, protection, and their clothes did not wear out in the desert. Here Moses received the law the first time. All of this had already taken place by the time we get to Exodus 33:12. Yet, this passage betrays the fact that Moses still does not feel like He knows God very well!

Vs 12. "Then Moses said to the LORD, "See, You say to me, 'Bring up this people.' But You have not let me know whom You will send with me. Yet You have said, I know you by name, and you have also found grace in My sight."

Moses was not saying, "God, You did not tell me who or what other man is going to go with me." No, his question in the original language was more along the lines of, "You say that I have found grace in Your sight, but I do not even know who You are who is going to go with me!" Remember, God had already said to him in Exodus 3:12, "Go, I will be with you"
"And God said, I will be with you. And this will be the sign to you that it is I who have sent you." NIV

Personally, I think Moses was pretty wise to go up to God and tell Him, "Hey God, I do not know who You are, but I want to get to know You! You said that you know me and that I have found grace in Your sight." Moses was recounting to God what He had spoken to him before.

Then, Moses shifted gears in verse 13, *"Now therefore, I pray thee, if I have found grace in thy sight, show me now thy way, that I may know thee, that I may find grace in thy sight: and consider that this nation is thy people."* Moses said to God, "If I have found grace in Your sight, then You need to show me Your ways. Show me how You do things. Show me how You operate. Show me how You function so I can know who You are." That was pretty smart of Moses because to find these things out would be helpful. Then at least he would know how God functions in His Kingdom. Then Moses would be able to discern whether something he encountered was God at work or not!

As Christians, I wish we would do that too! It would be really helpful to find out more information about God's ways. Then we could at least be able to tell whether something is God at work or not. So many different things happen in church services and in the daily lives of Christians that are labeled " God", but are not really God at all. This is one reason why it is important to know God and how He does things!

Even though Moses requested to see God's ways, God did not do what he asked. Why? The ways of God are immeasurable. God did not show Moses how He made the universe, how He keeps things in their places, etc. It would have taken an eternity to show Moses all of His ways. Moses would still be on the mountain and the Israelites would have all died in the desert. Think of it!

I Will Give You Rest

However, God answered in verse 14, *"My presence shall go with thee, and I will give thee rest."* God says, " I am not going to show you how I operate, but what I will show you is that My presence

24

will go with you and where my presence is there is rest." Be sure to catch the meaning here. " I am not going to show you how I do things, but I will show you that when I am present, there will always be rest."

" Rest" means " to sit back, kick off your shoes, kick back, and relax." In fact, I tell people sometimes, " I have a word of prophecy for you. God wants you to relax!" Christians can be so uptight at times. We have all of these things we feel we need be to be doing all of the time. There are all kinds of formulas floating around in our heads that we feel we need to apply in order to get God to work for us. Listen to what God said to Moses. " When I am present and working, the result will always be rest." That means that rest is an environment produced when God is present.

Another shade of meaning for " rest" also applies. " Rest" also means, " to be in a state where you know that all investigation into your life has ceased." Imagine someone you trust walking up to you right now with a message stating that they have strong evidence that your life is under investigation by the secret police, the FBI or any other authority regarding a serious accusation. Furthermore, the investigators are now going through all of your private affairs, your business records, and your tax returns for the last decade. Their purpose is to find out whether or not you are one of those Bin Laden terrorist types. Your friend also lets you know that these authorities are interviewing all of your family and friends. He had already been interviewed before coming to see you. Then, after telling you all of this, he turns around on his way out the door and remarks, " Hey, enjoy the rest of your afternoon, and have a good nights rest!"

Even though you know in your heart that you have not done anything wrong intentionally, you are definitely not going to be able to rest much that afternoon, and you will certainly not have a good nights rest! You have just become aware of the fact that you are now under the scrutiny of someone in a position of authority who is trying to find something wrong in your life. Even though you have not done anything wrong intentionally, there is always the possibility that you did do something wrong unintentionally. Maybe you were the unknowing friend of some hoodlum or terrorist. Think about how that would feel. You cannot rest!

In the same way, it is true that you can never rest or experience the rest of God as a Christian as long as you believe that God is continually investigating your life to find something wrong! If your view of God includes Him continually looking for something wrong in your life, then you have a wrong view of God. The Word says that wherever He is and is busy working, the result will always be rest. You are able to sit back, relax, and let that heavy weight roll off your shoulders because you know that God is on your side. Now that is wonderful!

God Is With You

Verse 15 continues with Moses, *"If thy presence go not with me, carry us not up hence."* Basically, Moses said, "God, if that is true, then do not send us anywhere if You are not going to go with us!" I have made that my prayer too. Father, please do not let me go anywhere if You are not going to go with me! But He has promised that He will never leave us or forsake us. Hallelujah!

26

Rest in His Goodness

Dear friend, do you find yourself somewhere in life all stressed out and worried? Stop and take inventory of where you are and how you got there. Take a step back and be objective with yourself. Are you doing what God has called you to do? The truth may in fact be that you are not. Be encouraged—He still loves you! He is a good God! However, you will remain in this stressed out condition for as long as you are not functioning within the sphere of God's influence in your life. Will God leave you to just burn out if you are out of His will? No way! Rest assured knowing that He is and will do everything He can to bring you back into the center of His will. By this I do not mean that God will cause calamity and hardships to come into your life in order to work out His plan and purpose for your life. No! not at all. The Bible teaches us in Romans 2:17, that it is the goodness of God that leads us to repentance. God will do all He can do in and through His goodness, love and mercy to bring you back to His will for your life. He desires to fulfill every promise that He has ever made in your life.

If God is with you, what will be the result? Rest! You will have rest in your life. Does "rest" mean that things will never go wrong? No! It means that right there in the middle of all hell breaking loose, you will have rest. As everything hits the fan, so to speak, you are in rest. Rest has to do with your internal condition, not your external circumstances. Rest is your heart's condition.

Known By His Rest

Rest is what God's people will be known by. Verse 16 continues, *"For wherein shall it be known here that I and thy people have found grace in thy sight? Is it not in that thou goest with us? So shall we be separated, I and thy people, from all the people that are upon the face of the earth."* Moses asked, "How will the people of God be known?" The word "separate" means "to be distinguished." "How will God's people be distinguished from the rest of the people on the face of the earth?"

I believe that many of us in the Church have perverted this reality in the past decade or two. We have proclaimed, "The people of God will be distinguished by their moral conduct. We will be known for our impeccable moral character." I used to preach that! From the pulpit, I could expound with the best of them, "Brother, you need to live right. You need to do right. Be the example of the Kingdom of God to this lost world. Show these people dying in their sins what a true Christian is like. Let your good works so shine as a bright light for all to see!" That is all well and good, until somebody has a public moral failure. When an exemplary Christian such as a well-known pastor or television personality, a famous entertainer or athlete falls, or when the skeletons come out of the closet, most of us are pretty disappointed and the world just carries on thinking that believers are a bunch of hypocrites.

Your morality is not what will set you apart as a man or a woman of God! David was a man after God's own heart. He was distinguished as a man of God above many other men. Did David's morality determine that? No way! Does that mean that we can just live in sin and get away with it? No way! I am just telling you that it is not your morality that is going to communicate to the world that you are set apart as one of God's people. I know some people who

28

live a much better moral life as unbelievers than many others do as Christians. So what do we say now?

The people of God are distinguished from the people of this world because in the midst of crisis, you can have peace. In the midst of turmoil, you can be at rest. The world will look at you dumbfounded. "The whole world is falling apart. The terrorists are sending anthrax in envelopes all over the world, but you are not worried? The next bomb could very well go off in your neighborhood, but you are not anxious about it? What gives?"

Why Must I Be Afraid?

Not long after the terrorist events occurring in the USA on September 11, 2001, I was on a ministry trip abroad. Many people came to me during that time, both Europeans and Americans, asking,

"Are you flying on the airplanes?"

I told them the truth. "Yeah, why?"

"Aren't you afraid?" they would ask.

"Why must I be afraid? Why must I stop doing what God wants me to do just because there are some terrorists in the world? That is exactly what the terrorists want."

The devil is the original terrorist. He works on the same principle of fear. He wants to scare you into not trusting God. If he can get you to submit to his terror tactics once, he will try to paralyze you for good. Sure my wife was a little nervous when I left, but I was not about to be slowed down in sharing this good news all around the world!

The "rest" of God governs my life. I am not going to let these things stop me. If that airplane falls, guess who will survive? Me! You may say, "Now Arthur, that is a bit idealistic, isn't it?" Hey, if I cannot believe for God's protection as I endeavor to do His will, then what are we doing here anyway? Do you know what? The plane might fall and I may not survive but at least I went down believing in Him!

Paul had this "rest" of God working in his life. He said, "Whichever way, I am a winner! Hallelujah! Kill me, I win. Beat me, I win. Let me go, I win." Now that is rest! How will you be distinguished? You are a person of rest in your workplace. When things go wrong, you are at peace. When people are being laid off because business is bad, you are in rest. Everybody else is chewing their nails down to the quick. You can just sit there and declare, "Even if I lose my job, God's got a better one for me." Why? "He is on my side! I am always a winner!" That's you! You are distinguished by His "rest"!

Glory and Goodness

Verse 17 continues, *"And the LORD said unto Moses, I will do this thing also that thou hast spoken: for thou hast found grace in my sight, and I know thee by name."* This is God agreeing to give us rest.

Moses made another request in verse 18. *"I beseech thee, show me thy glory."* Moses asked God to show him the fullness of who He is. The word for "glory" right there means "the totality of God, the splendor of who He is." He asked, "Show me who You are!"

God replied in verse 19, *"I will make all my goodness pass before thee, and I will proclaim the name of the LORD before thee."* What? Didn't God hear Moses' question? Moses wanted to see God's glory, but God said that He would parade His goodness before him. We have to recognize here that God was saying, "My glory and My goodness are one and the same!"

If we want to know the Father heart of God, then we need to make a decision today about God's goodness. According to the Word, either God is good or He is not. Friend, what do you say? What will your view and opinion be? I say He is good. His goodness is not merely something He does, but it is who He is. It does not matter how or when you come into contact with God, you come into contact with good. God told Moses, "All My goodness will pass before you." Moses was about to behold God in all His goodness!

Your Condition and His Nature

I really want you to understand what the Bible is saying here about God being good. Imagine that I am standing before you behind a wooden pulpit. Do you have that picture in your mind? Okay. I can call this physical object in front of me a "pulpit." I could also refer to the pulpit as "this wood" since it is wood. Wood is what the pulpit is. It is made out of wood. I want you to make

31

this connection. God is good and good is God!

Let us just say that I leave the room and come back a whole week later. When I return, let us say that I have not spent any time all week with God. I attended no meetings with other believers. I have not read the Bible, or even prayed one bit all week long. In fact I am backslidden, depressed and disappointed. When I walk into the room, I stride over to the pulpit and I touch it. I come into contact with the pulpit. Is it still a pulpit? Yes. Is it still wood? Yes.

Okay, this time, let us say that I walk in the room as a super-spiritual Christian. I have been fasting and praying all week long. I read the entire New Testament in the past seven days. Everything is going good and my heart is full of praise! I walk into the room and reach out to touch the pulpit. Am I touching a pulpit? Yes. Am I touching wood? Yes.

So it is easy to see that the condition of my life does not change the pulpit. The condition of my morality does not change the wood. The condition of my heart, or my emotions, does not change the pulpit. Why? It is a pulpit and it is wood, independent from me.

Why do you think that the condition of your life changes God? God is good. It does not matter if your condition is good or not. Whenever you come into contact with God, you come into contact with good. He is good! Your condition does not change Him.

Now, if I could take the wood out of the pulpit, would the pulpit still exist? No, it would not. If God's goodness could be taken away from Him or be separated from Him, then God would not exist either. Wow! In order for God to not be good to people, He would have to cease to be God. You need to get a hold of this truth! It will revolutionize your relationship with your heavenly Father. This is what His Word communicates to us!

You must allow the view and opinion that you have of God to be transformed to agree with His Word. God is good! Let the image in your heart of Him be shaped by this truth. If God were anything but good to you right now, He would cease to exist. It does not matter when you come to Him or how you come to Him, He will be good to you. When you come into contact with God, you come into contact with goodness!

Four

A Schizophrenic God?

A nd he said, I will make all my goodness pass before thee, and I will proclaim the name of the LORD before thee; and will be gracious to whom I will be gracious, and will show mercy on whom I will show mercy. And he said, Thou canst not see my face: for there shall no man see me, and live. And the LORD said, Behold, there is a place by me, and thou shalt stand upon a rock: And it shall come to pass, while my glory passeth by, that I will put thee in a cleft of the rock, and will cover thee with my hand while I pass by: And I will take away mine hand, and thou shalt see my back parts: but my face shall not be seen.

Here in Exodus 33:19, God states, *"(I) will be gracious to whom I will be gracious, and will show mercy on whom I will show mercy."*

A Schizophrenic God?

This is a scripture that has been used and abused by religious interpretations. People think this says, "You see, God is God. He alone decides who He will be good to and who He will be gracious to. There are some people that He will not be gracious to and others that He will be gracious to." Is that what this verse is saying? No, not at all! Let us take off our religious prejudices and listen to what God is really saying: "I will show you My goodness. When you see who I really am, you will not be the one to determine who I can be good to and who I cannot be good to."

I am amazed at Christians who get disappointed with God because He is good to people that they think He should not be good to. Has this ever happened to you? We say, "God, I know their life! I know they took money out of the offering bucket last week instead of putting any in. I know that they got drunk last weekend and hit their spouse." Then, God is good to them anyway. It just baffles a religious mind that God is all good!

Killer Glory?

Verse 20 gets really interesting. God is still speaking. *"Thou canst not see my face: for there shall no man see me, and live."* This is another verse of scripture that has been interpreted and seen wrong over and over again. Are you familiar with the movie, "Raiders of the Lost Ark?" It's okay if you have seen that movie. You can still be a Christian and watch a movie. God certainly does not mind if you want to watch a movie now and again.

Do you remember the scene when they open the Ark of the Covenant and the "glory of God" comes out into the room? The good guy, named Indiana Jones, tells all of his buddies, "Close your eyes. Don't look upon the 'glory of God' because the scripture says you will die!" No, the scripture never says that you will die. It just says that you will not live!

What is the difference? This is the difference. In the motion picture, they depict this whole thing where the Germans have been trying to get the Ark of the Covenant to use as a good luck charm during World War II. The "glory of the Lord" is shining all around, angelic beings are flying around, the wicked soldiers' skin melts off and their blood and guts start running all over the place. They die a horrible death!

I have always asked myself the question, "Where did Hollywood get their ideas from to make a movie like that?" I believe it was because many Christians have depicted God to be that way. "Buddy, if you do not do what God wants you to do, He is going to get you!" So the film makers fictitiously portrayed the "glory of God" slaughtering sinners. I want to tell you in the strongest way I can, this is the DIRECT OPPOSITE of the true effects of the glory of God!

I Need You Here On Earth!

Getting back to the Bible passage we were discussing, *"Thou canst not see my face: for there shall no man see me, and live"* (Vs 20). Let me explain to you what it means. Have you ever heard of a fellow by the name of Enoch? The Bible says that he walked with God. One day, he went on a walk with God and never came back. I am sure that Enoch was enjoying his walk with God that day. The presence of the Lord was so strong, God's goodness was so tangible. I bet he said to himself, "I am going to sneak a peek." He looked into the face of God's goodness and was so overwhelmed, and overcome by it all, that he just never came back. Why would anyone want to keep living down here after beholding Him? He is the most attractive Person in the Universe!

So God told Moses, "Moses, you will not look upon My face because I need you here on earth to deliver these people. If you look upon My face, you will not come back." Verses 21-23 continue the Lord's answer, *"Behold, there is a place by me, and thou shalt stand upon a rock: and it shall come to pass, while my glory passeth by, that I will put thee in a cleft of the rock, and will cover thee with my hand while I pass by: and I will take away mine hand, and thou shalt see my back parts: but my face shall not be seen."* Another translation says, "My backside." I am not trying to be funny here. I am just telling you that this is exactly what God did!

God said to Moses, "You are not going to look at My face. I am going to show you My least comely side." That least attractive side was so gloriously powerful that when Moses came down from the mountain, his face shone so with the glory of God that the Israelites told him to cover his face because they were afraid. God told Moses, "I will show you My least comely side because that is about all you can take!"

In Exodus 33 God told Moses what He was going to do. In Exodus 34 was when He actually did it. Verse 4 describes Moses going up the mountain with two new stone tablets. Verse 5 says, "And the LORD descended in the cloud, and stood with him there, and proclaimed the name of the LORD." Notice how there was no hesitation in God coming down to Moses. Moses did not first have to try to get the "atmosphere" right. He did not have to tear down the strongholds so that God could come through. God came right to him!

The Lord Passed By

"And the LORD passed by before him, and proclaimed, The LORD, The LORD God, merciful and gracious, longsuffering, and abundant in goodness and truth" (Vs 6). God passed by Moses and showed His backside, His least comely part. Proclamation of His character happened simultaneously during this tremendous moment. Who is our Father? The Lord God, merciful and gracious. He is full of mercy and grace! Now, if He is full of mercy and grace that means there is no room for anything else! Longsuffering. I am so glad for that! He had better be when He deals with me because I make a lot of mistakes! Abounding in goodness and truth. Wow!

"Keeping mercy for thousands" (Vs 7). One of the translations I have *(The Holy Bible From Ancient Eastern Manuscripts) (George M Lamsa)* renders this phrase, *"keeping mercy for thousands of generations."* That really opens it up! "I will keep My mercy for thousands of generations."

"...forgiving iniquity and transgression and sin..." Our Father is forgiving. He forgives your iniquity, transgression, and sin. Notice how God covers all three areas just to make sure you do not think there was something you were not forgiven of! Hallelujah!

38

A Schizophrenic God?

"…and that will by no means clear the guilty; visiting the iniquity of the fathers upon the children, and upon the children's children, unto the third and to the fourth generation." This section of verse 7 has been used in the church to bring forth teaching that has kept people in such bondage. I would like to challenge the interpretation that you are probably most familiar with and offer an alternative for your consideration. It does not matter who told you the popular interpretation that you have heard before. Please study this out for yourself! The popular interpretation goes like this: God said, "This is who I am. I am a God full of mercy and grace. I keep mercy for thousands of generations. I am a forgiving God. I forgive iniquity, transgression and sin. But do you know what? I will not let you go free. In fact, I am going to pass all these results of your sin down to your children and your children's children. I am going to make them suffer!" I do not know about you, but it seems to me that this interpretation makes God seem schizophrenic! However, we know that God is not schizophrenic, so how does this square up?

Whenever we find verses like this in the Bible where what is being said goes totally against what God has just revealed, either we are interpreting it wrongly, or it has been interpreted wrongly by the translators. I used to skip that particular verse. Have you ever done that? I was confused. "God, this does not make sense to me. How can You say that You forgive me of all my sins, iniquities and transgressions; and then You are going to punish me and my descendants for them. I don't get it!"

Digging Deeper

Over some months I decided I had to find out what this

meant. So I dug into the Hebrew. No, I am not a Hebrew scholar, but I did what I knew to do for word studies. In the phrase, *"clear the guilty"* notice that in the King James Version *"the guilty"* is in italics. This means that these two words are not in the original language, which implies that God did not say them. The passage then changes slightly to read, "...by no means clear; visiting the iniquity of the fathers upon..." This clue was encouraging, but the next one broke this mystery wide open for me.

The fellow who wrote "The Living Bible," did a study like I did on this particular passage. He placed a little note there in his version saying that he studied the actual literal translation and it says, *"I am Jehovah who shows the steadfast love to many thousands by forgiving their sins or else I refuse to clear the guilty and require that the father's sins be punished on the sons, grandsons, and even on the later generations."* Now what does this mean? God said, "Listen to Me, this is who I am. I am showing you My goodness. I am a God of mercy. I am a God of forgiveness. I forgive all your transgressions, your sins, your iniquities. I blot them out because if I do not do that, I will have to pass the sins of the fathers on to the children. But because I am a good God, I will not do it!"

Exodus 33:7 has been used to preach a message of the father's sins being passed on to their children. Nowadays, they call it "generational curses." As Christians, we have swallowed this errant teaching for years. I contend that this is not what God was saying in this passage. I do not believe that there is any foundation whatsoever for the teaching of generational curses to New Testament believers.

A Schizophrenic God?

2 Corinthians 5:17 proclaims, *"Therefore if any man be in Christ, he is a new creature: old things are passed away; behold, all things are become new."* The J.B. Phillips translation says it this way, *"If any man be in Christ, he is a new creature, old things have passed away, behold everything is fresh and new."* Are you in Christ? Are you "any man"? If you are in Christ, the old things are passed away. They have passed away. Would you call that generational curse an old thing? Yes? Then it has passed away. You cannot get past that verse. You cannot teach generational curses in the New Testament.

New Testament people are exempt from such things. Paul tells us in 1 Timothy 1:3-4 to stay away from fables and endless genealogies. You cannot teach generational curses without going into genealogies. Jesus changes each of us individually as we draw near and start to be whole in Him. He wants to change the view that we have of Him and of ourselves. When we change the view we have, we will begin to see who we are. We will start to see the hope and the calling of our lives. This Bible is a portrait of who God is. It is also a mirror of who we are in Him. When we see ourselves as New Testament people through what Jesus did on the cross, the revelation He has for us really begins to open up.

Let us pray together. Wonderful Lord Jesus, I come before You today realizing how much I have misinterpreted Your character. Sometimes, it is even hard for me to believe that You really are this good. Father, I ask You to give me a spirit of wisdom and revelation in the knowledge of You that the eyes of my understanding may be enlightened to see You for who You really are.

Thank You that as I see You more accurately and clearly, Your Word and Your Spirit will transform me from the inside out. I will be changed from glory to glory into Your image and likeness as I behold You day by day.

Thank You for giving me this glimpse of Your goodness! I make a decision today to choose to see You as a good God. Moses was overwhelmed by the mere sight of the backside of Your goodness, how much more am I, as Your child, in love with you. My face is unveiled as I behold Your glory! Transform me today!

Fight the Good Fight

I just sense by the Spirit of God that you might be wrestling right now with some thoughts like, "Well, if I don't believe that God is going to beat me up, how will I be motivated to serve Him?"

My friend, I just want to ask you to keep on looking to His goodness. Keep on believing. As Christians, this is a walk of faith that we are on. Paul writes to us to fight the good fight of faith. You and I need to fight the good fight of always trusting that God is good. God will be good to you no matter what. Even in the midst of your failures, Your Father will be good to you.

You may even be going through some seasons of change in your life right now. You feel uncomfortable and unsettled. I want to encourage you to keep stepping out into the true walk of faith today. Allow the Holy Spirit to persuade your heart of His goodness. It does not matter what successes, or what failures, are happening in your life right now. God is good!

God wants to be good to you! He is merciful and gracious. He is forgiving. Yes, perhaps you have made some mistakes, but He is greater.

Just where you are, lift up your hands and begin to worship Him. Do this as a sign of opening up yourself to Him. You are no longer afraid of Him. He is definitely not a God to be afraid of. Respect? Yes! What loving Father wants His kids to be afraid to come near Him? You do not need to try to measure up to some standard of performance in your life before you can draw close. No! Jesus did it for you. You are in Him. Draw near! Enjoy His manifest presence! Hallelujah!

Five

Made To See

A nd in front of the throne there was also what looked like a transparent glassy sea, as if of crystal. And around the throne, in the center at each side of the throne, were four living creatures (ones, beings) who were full of eyes in front and behind [with intelligence as to what is before and at the rear of them] - (Revelation 4:6) AMP

In The Throne Room

I would like to look at what would normally be considered a somewhat obscure scripture. I want to draw your attention to some fascinating realities alluded to here. John saw these things when he looked into the throne room of God.

Notice how these living beings are described. Verses 7 and 8, *"The first living creature (one, being) was like a lion, the second living creature like an ox, the third living creature had the face of a man, and the fourth living creature [was] like a flying eagle. And the four living creatures, individually having six wings, were full of eyes all over and within [underneath their wings]; and day and night they never stop saying, Holy, holy, holy is the Lord God Almighty (Omnipotent), Who was and Who is and Who is to come"* AMP. This verse clearly elaborates upon the fact that they are full of eyes. I want you to see that this whole passage of scripture talks about "eyes" often. These beings are *"full of eyes in front and behind."* These creatures have the ability to perceive what is before and behind them.

This tells us that these creatures were made for a distinct purpose. These creatures were made to see something! They are full of eyes in the front. They are full of eyes in the back. In verse 8 we are told that they *"were full of eyes all over and within"* (AMP) and each one had six wings. Although you and I have never seen a creature like this, we can tell from this information that they were made to see something even while flying!

Perceptions of Reality

As I have already said before, very few people relate to God for who He really is. We tend to relate to the "God" we perceive Him to be. Our beliefs and perceptions as human beings can change over time, even though the specific object of our beliefs and perceptions does not change.

Do you remember places and events from your childhood? I remember one of the houses I lived in as a boy. From birth to around seven years old, I grew up in this particular house in Crosby (located on the south side of Johannesburg in South Africa). I remember the perceptions I had about this house. It had a huge veranda or stoop area. I recall how big it was because I used to play in there often, especially in the passage or hallway that went to the bedrooms. The house originally belonged to the South African Railways. My dad used to work for the railways. The bathroom was at the end of this long passage. There were black and white tiles on the floor. Everything was so huge and long to me back then!

As a grown man, I returned to that area about ten years ago. Out of curiosity, I visited that particular old house where I had spent the first few years of my life. All the memories came flooding back to me on the way over. However, I was mildly shocked to see that it was not the same as I had perceived it before. Upon my arrival, I exclaimed, "This is not how I remember it!" What I had experienced as a small boy as a veritable palace had shrunk into a small, dinky little house.

Now, you and I know that houses do not shrink. However, my perception of that place had changed! What seemed to me to be huge as a child became tiny as an adult. The way that I experienced that house as a child also differed from the way I experienced it as an adult. The last time I had been there was when I was about seven years old. Now that I am an adult, my perception and experience of it changed!

As Christians, we have a perception of who God is, but that does not necessarily mean our image of Him is really who He is. Do you understand what I am saying? None of us can really say, "I know who God is in His entirety!" We have to go to the Bible and allow His Word to change our perceptions through the power of the Holy Spirit in order to have a fuller, more accurate picture of Him.

I Do Not Know This "God"

A couple came and joined our church while I was still pastoring a church in Middelburg, South Africa several years ago. I had met them previously and had known them for a while. I knew that the wife had been a Christian for a long time. I did not know how long she had been involved in church and with God, but it had been quite a while. They started regularly attending our church.

One morning about the third time they came for Sunday services, I ministered on the goodness of God. It was just a simple message revealing from the Word who God really is as a good God. I endeavored to paint understandable pictures of His goodness so that the hearers could get a handle on what I was sharing (people perceive and remember things more in pictures, not words).

Every time I glanced over in this couple's direction, the lady looked utterly flabbergasted. Her mouth hung wide open all the time while I was preaching. Her husband kept looking at her and then looking at me. It was like a tennis match! He looked at her with wonder and amazement, and then he would look at me.

After the service, the congregation was busy having a great time of fellowship like we usually do. I had joined in until I felt someone tugging on my shirt. When I turned around it was this lady. She had been bawling her eyes out. Tears and mascara had intermingled their way down her wet and distraught face. There, standing behind her, was her husband. His eyes bulged out (you know how men are when they want to and do not want to cry—all at the same time). They looked at me in that condition and I thought, "Oh my, what has happened?"

So I asked, "What is the matter?"
"No, no, no! I need to speak to you," she blubbered in between sobs.

I led them into a corner gently inquiring what the problem was.

The lady continued by stammering, "No, no, no! Listen." Then she caught her breath and continued, "I just want to tell you that I do not know this "God" that you are talking about."

Trying to console her, I responded, "Well, you know. We all have our misconceptions,"

"No, no, no! You don't understand!" she blurted out. "I grew up in a pastor's home. I am the daughter of a minister. Yet, I have never ever seen God the way that you spoke of Him today."

Her bulging-eyed husband piped in, "Neither have I!" This precious couple had come into contact with the revelation of the goodness of God and it turned their whole view of Him upside down, or should I say the right way up!

Nothing Like I Thought You Were

Friend, you might be saved and going to heaven, but I want you to grasp the fact that just because you have been involved in church, have read your Bible, and have professed to be a Christian for a period of time does not automatically mean that you have a correct picture of who God is. Please, I want you to understand. I am not necessarily claiming to have "it all" either. However, I do know that somehow God has ministered into my heart some powerful truths pertaining to knowing God for who He really is. He has utterly and completely transformed my life!

You see, for most of the years I have been a Christian, I had a totally wrong view of God. The reason this made me so miserable is because as human beings we become transformed into the image of the "God" we see. You become like the "God" you serve. My "God" was angry and hard to please. I had become a person who was angry and hard to please. He has freed me from a wrong image of Himself and has given me the ability to minister these same liberating truths to others as well. This is my heart's desire for you!

Another family came and joined our church about eight years ago. This man and his wife became very good friends with my wife and I. We started doing things together socially like going out to dinner. One December, they invited us down to their house at the coast. We stayed there for three weeks having great fun together.

We were eating a meal together one day during this time, when the lady looked up at us and commented, "Do you know what, Arthur and Cathy? I just want to tell you something. You are nothing like I thought you would be!"

Naturally, I was curious. So I asked, "Well…why?"

"You are just totally different to the way I expected you to be," she continued. "I knew about you and I had also heard about you from other people. This view I had of you is nothing like the way you are."

I believe that this lady's comments concerning my wife and I will be true of many of us when we get to heaven one day and see God the Father for who He really is. Perhaps after being there for a couple of millennium, we will go up to God and say, "Daddy, You are nothing like I thought You would be."

Do you know what? I do not necessarily want to have to get

to that place. In fact, my preference would be to arrive in heaven saying, "Yeah, He is exactly how I imagined Him to be." He has given us His Word. We have the Holy Spirit to lead us into all truth and to reveal Jesus Who revealed the Father. You do not have to wait until you get to heaven one day to see Him for Who He really is!

Holy, Holy, Holy!

Okay, so what does all of this have to do with the scripture in Revelation 4:6-8? Well, I am glad you asked! These creatures are around the throne of God. These creatures with eyes everywhere were created to see something. I had read these verses many times. In my inquisitive mind, which constantly asks questions, I would wonder about these creatures that are covered in eyes and rotating around the throne of God. They were made to see something. The last part of verse 8 tells us that every time they rotate around the throne of God, day in and day out, they cry, *"Holy, holy, holy is the Lord God Almighty (Omnipotent), Who was and Who is and Who is to come"* AMP

I do not know about you, but forever seemed to me to be a long time! Just think of being a creature who will forever cry, *"Holy, holy, holy is the Lord God Almighty (Omnipotent), Who was and Who is and Who is to come."* I thought, "Somewhere in there that ought to get just a little bit boring!" Think about it! They have been doing it forever. They will be doing it forever. That is all they say all day long. One day I was reading that and in my mind I thought, "How boring!"

Just then the Holy Spirit spoke to me asking, "Do you know why they say that? It is because every time they rotate, they see a new aspect of the goodness and mercy of God that they have never seen before. They see a brand new shade of the love and glory of God that they have never ever seen before. This revelation causes them to cry out, 'Holy, holy, holy!'"

Our God is so awesome that there always was and will be four beings around His throne that will never see the end of God's goodness and mercy. They will never ever get to the end of God's love and grace. Every time they rotate, they see an aspect that they had never seen before and it impacts them! Every time they do see, they are so deeply impressed that their reaction is to worship Him!

How is it then that for so many years we in the Church have tried to beat people into worshiping and serving God? If we will begin to reveal who He really is to people, their natural reaction and response will be to start worshiping Him.

Personal, Intimate, Experiential Knowledge

As we go through this study, I will repeat certain key scriptures. I am doing this on purpose so that the truths that are contained in them will sink deeper into your life by repetition. With this in mind, I want to go back to Ephesians chapter 1. This time, let us look at it in the Amplified Version.

Verse 16 (AMP) says, *"I do not cease to give thanks for you, making mention of you in my prayers."* Notice the frequency with which Paul makes this request. He does not cease praying this prayer. This means that he prays these same grateful requests for wisdom and understanding often.

Continuing with verse 17 (AMP), *"[For I always pray to] the God of our Lord Jesus Christ, the Father of glory, that He may grant you a spirit of wisdom and revelation [of insight into mysteries and secrets] in the [deep and intimate] knowledge of Him."* It is a prayer that can be answered again and again because, as we saw from Revelation 4:6-8, this revelation has no end!

As a pastor and a traveling teacher, this is what I continually pray for those I minister to. I pray that our local church body, and all the believers I come in contact with, will become shining lights to the rest of the world. I am trusting God that we will illuminate our countries and our cities with the beauty of who God really is. Our desire is for others to come to the knowledge of God. Some may say, "Well, everybody knows about God." That is not what I am talking about here. We need to come to the knowledge of God. There is an important difference!

The Greek word used in this passage for the word "knowledge" is the word "ginosko." It is interesting to note that this particular word for "knowledge" is not used anywhere else in the Bible, except for Paul's epistles and Peter's writings. This word is not used in the Gospels. It is not talking about just knowing about something. The root meaning is "to recognize a thing to be what it really is." We are not talking about a mere perception of something, but to actually come to the realization of what it really is. This word also denotes "exact or full knowledge." It is "knowledge that comes out of intimacy and directly influences the one who knows."

Understanding the meaning of this word "knowledge" sheds additional light on our scripture passage. Paul says, "I want you to come to the full realization. I ask that God would give you a spirit of knowledge and insight into finding out who He really is. When you find out who God really is, that intimate knowledge will affect the person who knows." Hallelujah! This is the kind of "knowledge" being talked about here, not just merely a knowing about. This is the kind of knowledge that God Your Father wants you to have of Him!

Six

Grace To Know Your Father

J esus came to earth to give us an accurate picture of who God is. He taught us to pray saying, *"After this manner therefore pray ye: Our Father which art in heaven…"* (Matthew 6:9). Do you realize how revolutionary these words were to the people who heard Jesus teach them? You have to understand that up until Jesus arrived on the scene and started ministering, there really was no concept in this world of God being our Father. No concept whatsoever!

People had theology. They knew about God, but intimate knowledge of Him so personal that it deeply affected the heart of the "knower" was conspicuously absent! You see theology can give you an academic degree. It might even be able to give you a good job or position of some kind. However, when you know God the way Paul reveals in Ephesians 1:16-17, that kind of knowledge changes your heart. Really, this is what God is after in His people. This intimate, personal, experiential, life-changing knowledge of Him is true Christianity. Knowing Him!

When Jesus said, "Our Father," He was truly saying that God is our Father. This is what enraged the religious people so much that they wanted to kill Him. Until Jesus came, people had no concept of God being Father. People knew God as an angry God who needed to be appeased by doing good and trying to keep Him happy all the time. When Jesus came, He taught and demonstrated who God really is and that He is our heavenly Father.

Every time you and I say the word, "Father," each one of us has a different concept of what that means based upon our perceptions and experiences. To some people, a "father" is a callous, harsh, hard to please person. To others, a "father" is a drunkard who did not care for his kids, but hid himself in a bottle of booze. There are many other potential concepts of what a "father" is like. However, we must go to God's Word and allow His word to show us who God our Father really is. You see, when we do not relate to God for who He really is, we cannot experience Him for who He really is. I decided in my heart long ago that I was finished with serving a "God" where there is no experience of Him. Let me encourage you, I have not been disappointed! God is so real that He wants you to not only know about Him, but for you to know Him and experience Him for who He really is.

Grace: The Ability of God

"Simon Peter, a servant and apostle (special messenger) of Jesus Christ, to those who have received (obtained an equal privilege of) like precious faith with ourselves in and through the righteousness of our God and Savior Jesus Christ" 2 Peter 1:1 AMP Peter is talking to you and me. We are those who have obtained like precious faith through the righteousness of God in Jesus Christ, are we not? Then that means he is writing this for our benefit!

Verse 2 continues, *"May grace (God's favor) and peace (which is perfect well-being, all necessary good, all spiritual prosperity, and freedom from fears and agitating passions and moral conflicts) be multiplied to you in [the full, personal, precise, and correct] knowledge of God and of Jesus our Lord"* (AMP).

Grace! What is grace? "Grace" is not that little girl you once met long ago. God's grace is not just His "unmerited favor," even though most people who were trained in Sunday school will immediately and automatically spit that out as the definitive answer when asked. In meditating upon this concept of grace, I made a startling discovery. "Unmerited favor" is how grace comes, but it is not what grace is. Do you see it? Grace comes unmerited and unearned out of God's favorable disposition toward us, but how it comes does not really describe what it is. So then, we are still left with the question, "What is grace, anyway?"

According to the Strong's dictionary, charis (khar'-ece); graciousness (as gratifying), of manner or act (abstract or concrete; literal, figurative or spiritual; *especially the divine influence upon the heart...,):* This is talking about "Ability or Influence". God's grace exercises a divine influence or ability upon the heart of man, and it is an enabling power. The best way that I would define grace is that it is God's ability that has a divine influence upon the heart of man. Grace is God's ability working in and through me. When I started to see this, I realized why I was not able to live the life that I thought Christians ought to live. I had never put any kind of draw upon the grace of God. I had thought that it was all up to my ability to perform. I had not been allowing grace to work in my heart to enable me to live His life.

Peace and Emotional Stability

"Grace and peace be multiplied unto you through the knowledge of God, and of Jesus our Lord" (2 Peter 1:2). Have you ever realized that grace and peace travel together? They do! Without grace, you cannot have peace. Without God starting to work in your life by enabling you to do that which you naturally cannot do, you cannot have peace. Grace is God's ability. Peace is emotional stability. Both are absolutely essential to truly live the Christian life!

How are they multiplied to us? By the knowledge of God! In the Amplified version, we can easily see that same Greek word at work, *"…in [the full, personal, precise, and correct] knowledge of God and of Jesus our Lord"* (2 Peter 1:2b). We receive grace (God's ability to influence our hearts) and peace (emotional stability) by having an intimate knowledge of God and, therefore, experiencing Him to the degree that this intimate knowledge affects us!

Godly ability and emotional stability come when we have a correct and intimate knowledge of who God really is! May I make an observation? I do not mean to be disrespectful of His Body, but the parts of the church that I have become acquainted with for the last twenty plus years seem to have more emotionally unstable people than stable ones. Now this could be because there are many people in the church who are emotionally unstable because they might have been saved out of a messy, emotionally dysfunctional and worldly life. However, even those individuals who would truly have fallen into this category should not have stayed this way for very long after coming into the church. Think about it! If you were coming to church services as an emotional wreck, surely after a couple of years of being in the community of faith you would cross over into stability. If we preachers were really delivering the message of the Gospel in the way that Jesus did, we would be seeing more emotional wrecks become emotional rocks, after all this is called the Gospel of Peace. You are not supposed to stay in a place of instability. God's will is for you to move on by grace to peace!

Personally, I came to a place in my life after almost ten years of being a Christian where I said, "Listen, this stuff does not work. I am still struggling with the same junk as the first day I got saved! Why?" Well, the knowledge I had of God was incorrect knowledge. I was experiencing the fact that incorrect knowledge and unbelief of who God is was short circuiting His grace from working in my life. I know firsthand how incorrect knowledge of who God is hinders peace from taking root in your life. God's grace and peace cannot come to you through incorrect knowledge of Him.

A Funny Cheque

Years ago, I used to do conferences together with a good friend of mine and one time we held a conference in a place called Pinetown (near Durban, South Africa). The meetings took place all week long, from Sunday through Friday. I remember the Thursday morning of the conference. A lady came up and handed me a cheque for R172.63

After seeing the bewildered look on my face regarding the amount, she told me, "I want to give you this cheque." I asked her, "Do you want me to put it in the offering?"

"No, no! I want to give YOU this cheque."

I replied, "Thank you very much." The puzzled look on my face betrayed the questions that I was pondering in my heart. It struck me as such a funny amount! Most people would not

60

normally write out a gift cheque for R172.63. They would make it out for R172 or R200.

She continued, "I noticed that you are looking at the amount. Let me explain something to you, Arthur. I have been a Christian for almost twenty years. When I became a Christian I went to church, and started going through the normal Christian ranks. I have been through every counseling course and every intercession class. I have even been through deliverance too! Let me tell you something, for the last ten years I had to go and be under the care of a psychiatrist. I have never told my pastor this because he would flip out if he found out I was going to a psychiatrist!"

Ten years! So I asked her, motioning to the cheque, "Then, what is this?"

"This week, after sitting and hearing the good news, the knowledge and experience I have received of God's love, grace, mercy and goodness has completely changed my life. For the first time in many, many years I have peace again. I will never have to go to another psychiatrist again! I was scheduled to see him tomorrow. This is the cheque I would have given to him for his services."

I saw this lady again two years later. She had totally recovered and her whole family got saved through the influence of her life changing experience of getting to know God for who He really is.

When you start to see God for who He really is, that knowledge begins to work behind the scenes in your life. I know, I have been there! Sure, sure, everybody in the Body of Christ will intellectually agree saying, "We know God! God is our Father!" But listen, I know that many of us call Him by the title, "Father," but that does not mean that we actually and intimately relate to Him as Father! Reflect honestly for a moment upon your own current relationship with Him. Are you really experiencing Him as a good, loving Father?

All Things

1 Peter 1:3 says, *"For His divine power has bestowed upon us all things that [are requisite and suited] to life and godliness, through the [full, personal] knowledge of Him Who called us by and to His own glory and excellence (virtue)"* (AMP). I used to quote this verse only up to the end of the first section like this, He *"hath given unto us all things that pertain unto life and godliness"* (KJV). Boy, that was a shouting verse! The only problem was that I never saw any of those "things" that He gave me. I had learned that all you have to do is "confess" a verse in order to get the good stuff in it. So I confessed and confessed, but did not ever see anything.

Please do not misunderstand me! Confession has its place within your relationship with Him as you endeavor to shape your heart and renew your mind to His Word. Confession is a wonderful tool that helps you deposit and anchor the knowledge of God into your heart, but it is the revelation knowledge of God (not just merely scriptural facts about Him) that connect you as an individual believer to the promised "all things." Confession as a part of an intimate relationship with Him truly is powerful. However, confession for confession's sake ends up a work of the flesh when it does not really influence your heart to believe. Can you see it? I fell into that trap too. My head and my mouth were mechanically yapping away with knowledge about God, but relational knowledge of Him in my heart was what I really needed to access the "all things" He had given me!

What are those "all things?" God has given us all things that pertain to godliness! That word "godliness" means "God-likeness." The Lord has given us all things that will cause us to be God-like. I used to look in the mirror and remark, "Well, I know that I am human-like, but I am not God-like." Have you ever done that? It says here that according to "His divine power" He has given it to us. We are able to be God-like. How has he done it? God-likeness becomes a part of you when you have the knowledge of Him.

As a spiritual leader, I used to exhort my people strongly to, "Read the Word! Study the Word! Memorize the Word!" This is not what this passage is talking about. Have you ever noticed how religion and our flesh are always trying to get the means (confessing, reading, studying, memorizing, etc.) to take the place of the goal which is intimacy with Him? Of course, the Word will help us, but it is not the raw naked letters, words, and sentences of scripture that we are after. Really, it is the visual concepts that the Word paints within us that we are pursuing. We need God's accurate, life-giving, divine Word-pictures of Himself firmly established within our hearts. Through choosing to diligently interact with the Bible as an important part of our intimate relationship with the God of the Bible, we allow the Holy Spirit to paint beautiful portraits of our heavenly Father upon our hearts so that we can then experience Him. Experiencing God is our true aim and goal in confessing, reading, studying, and memorizing the Word!

The experience of your Christian life, and the quality of every area of that life (spiritually, emotionally, physically, etc.), is directly proportional to the intimate knowledge that you have of who God is. Let me say it another way so that I can be sure that I am bringing this truth home to you. The view and concept you have of God directly influences the quality of your life as a Christian.

God does not change. I am not asking you to imagine God in a way that He is not. Heaven forbid! But, I am telling you who God is, and the better you can "see" Him the better your ability will be to "experience" Him! Oh, how I pray that you understand this! You must face the reality that you may not have really seen God for who He truly is. The sooner and more honestly you do so, the quicker your relationship with your Father will improve! He is good! Yes, He is GOOD!!!

Seven

Believe In Your

Heart

P
roverbs 4:23 directs us to *"Keep thy heart with all diligence; for out of it are the issues of life."* This scripture admonishes us to keep our hearts. The importance of guarding our hearts cannot be understated, because this scripture tells us that the issues of life or the forces of life flow from the heart!

What is the "heart?" A person's "heart" is where their belief system is. Simply put, it is the part of you where you believe. *" That if thou shalt confess with thy mouth the Lord Jesus, and shalt believe in thine heart that God hath raised him from the dead, thou shalt be saved."* (Romans 10:9) Your heart is the part of you that understands concepts. Have you ever heard of something called the "subconscious mind?" We know it is a reality. Every person has a subconscious mind. The Bible simply calls it your "heart." When you study the Word of God, you will find that the same attributes psychiatrists and psychologists ascribe to the subconscious mind are the attributes that the Bible ascribes to the heart of man.

Proverbs 4:23 draws our attention to the need to protect our hearts because out of your heart will come the forces that drive your life. This means that the quality of your life today is directly related to what you believe and perceive in your heart. This is a scary thought. Most Christians do not like facing up to this fact because now they cannot just blame the devil for everything they do not currently like about their lives. It is not all the devil's fault that your life is messed up in the ways that it is. Many times it has nothing to do with the devil, or a mother-in-law, or the President, or the government, etc. The real issue has to do with what you are perceiving and believing in your heart! (I know that taking responsibility can sometimes be painful, but please do not stop reading this book here. I have more good news on the way!)

Two Powerful Heart Capabilities

As a human being, God has given you two capabilities that are exceptionally powerful toward affecting change within your life:

1. The ability to remember, and
2. The ability to imagine.

Now, I know that at this point many Christians will react violently saying, "Oh no! You cannot talk about imaginations in church. That is of the devil!" Well did the devil create you? No! God created you. Did God make you a human being with the ability to imagine? Yes! Therefore, your imagination is God given and has a godly purpose. (Remember, it was just "vain" imaginations that we were warned about, not "all" imaginations!) God gave you the ability to imagine for good purposes. He wants you to be able to see things that are not as though they are. Abraham did (Romans 4:17). God gave us these abilities!

Remembering and imagining have a common denominator in what is conversationally referred to as "visualization." That is just a fancy word to describe your ability to see with your inner man, to see with your heart. Religious Christians freak out when I use that particular word. They put their hands over their ears and act like they want to run out of the room screaming, " I knew you were a New Ager!"

When I started understanding and applying these principles and concepts, I saw such a change for good in my relationship with my heavenly Father and in my overall Christian life. Naturally, I began to share about remembering and imagining from the pulpit in different messages. I used some of these same words I just mentioned that happen to have an incidental overlap into the New Age realm. People started accusing me of being a New Age guru!

They would even say, "Oh, that is a New Age church." Really, all that happened was that the New Age movement stumbled upon some real truths about how we function as human beings made in God's image. They got busy putting an aspect of God's truth to work for themselves while we, the Body of Christ, continue to sit contently on our pews sucking our thumbs and wondering why we cannot materialize God's promises for our lives.

God made us to function a certain way, my friend! If you start to realize and apprehend how we function, you will be able to affect change in your life. God wants to change your life, but He has created you in a certain way. If you do not allow those things to become part of your change, then you are never going to truly change. As Christians, we have chosen to remain ignorant regarding these things, considering them to be evil because the heathen have discovered and used them. When will we recognize that all truth is God's truth? This includes visualization! He has given us the ability to remember and to imagine which enables us to see with the heart.

Set Your Affection

Colossians 3:1 proclaims, *" If ye then be risen with Christ, seek those things which are above, where Christ sitteth on the right hand of God."* Have you been risen with Christ? As born-again believers we have indeed died and been resurrected with Christ. Therefore, the answer is " Yes!" What is next?

Paul goes on *"Set your affection on things above, not on things on the earth"* (verse 2). The phrase " set your affection" translates from a Greek word meaning "to exercise your mind." There are some things that you are going to have to do in order for you to mature and grow up spiritually. You are going to have to exercise your mind!

This phrase, " set your mind," can also mean " to entertain." Let me illustrate this to you. As a kid I virtually grew up as an only child and I used to be good at entertaining myself. I love the beach and many times laying on my bed, I could be many miles away in my mind, on some beach by the sea. In fact, I could be anywhere in the world I wanted to be. How? Using my imagination. Through exercising my mind, I could travel to Durban beach in a heartbeat— the salty ocean air, the sound of a sea breeze, complete with the smells. Our imaginations are powerful!

This scripture tells us to exercise our mind and set them on things above where Christ is seated at the right hand of God. You cannot see that with your natural eyes. You have to see that with your imagination, with the eyes of your heart. There are dozens of scriptures in the Bible that teach us to see with the eyes of our heart. Some people choose to call it " the eye of faith."

You are going to have to exercise your mind in order to come to a greater understanding of who God is. You will have to choose to lay aside your old, distorted view so that you can embrace a more accurate view of Him. Exercise takes effort and work. The word " affection" lets us know that we are dealing not only with our thought realm, but also the realm of feeling. The

Word is discussing thoughts that involve emotions. It is talking about an experience. That is deeper than just a mere thought!

Seeing The Unseen

In 2 Corinthians 4:17-18 Paul says, *"For our light affliction, which is but for a moment, worketh for us a far more exceeding and eternal weight of glory; while we look not at the things which are seen, but at the things which are not seen: for the things which are seen are temporal; but the things which are not seen are eternal."* It is amazing how that works! I used to wonder, " How can I not look at the things which are seen? How can I not look at my circumstances? How can I not look?" Well, the Word says not to look on the things, which are seen. Why? Those things that are seen are " temporal." They are temporary, passing, fleeting, subject to change, but for a moment. However, the things that are not seen (and what we want to look at using the eyes of our heart) are eternal. Eternal means lasting, enduring, not subject to change, forever.

You have the capability to look upon things that are not seen in this physical, earthly world. Please understand I am not talking about seeing little angels flying around. I am constantly amazed at how Christians become so spooky. I am talking about seeing in your mind's eye, with the eyes of your heart, in your imagination. See the truth of who God really is and what He has done for you. Allow that to become more real to you than what is happening here in the physical world. My friend, when that happens, you are on the right track!

Believe in Your Heart

Isaiah says, *"Thou wilt keep him in perfect peace, whose mind is stayed on thee: because he trusteth in thee"* (Isaiah 26:3). Peace is emotional stability. The word in Hebrew there for "mind" literally means "your imagination." If you will keep your imagination, your affection, upon who God really is, He will keep you in perfect peace. Awesome!

Reality check! Does what you believe in your heart about God keep you in constant peace? Does your view of Him give you emotional stability? Or does it fill you with fear, condemnation and shame? Do your perceptions of God cause you to be afraid or to feel like you just are not measuring up? Do you feel that He does not really love you? Or fully accept you? (Note: I am talking about your feelings, not just the pat answers you have memorized and parroted for so many years! What do your feelings say?) If these are so, then what you believe about God is incorrect. This scripture plainly declares that if your mind is stayed on Him, He will keep you in perfect peace. Praise God!

God will never be real to us until we can have a healthy visual concept of who He is. I am not talking about just a mere theological concept. I am referring to your personal view of Him in your own heart. You and I must see Him for who He really is in His true nature and character. It is the only way we will be able to start to actually experience the life changing power of His grace, love, and mercy!

Closed Doors Opened

Years ago, God started revealing these truths to me. He began teaching me and showing me His love. Before, I had seen what the Word said, but did not have any experience of it personally. One day, I sat in my office reading from 1 Corinthians 13 (a.k.a. the Love Chapter). All of a sudden, the Holy Spirit started ministering to me saying, "Close your eyes." I did. Then, He continued, "I want you to visualize yourself in the throne room of God."

Do you know what? I could not do it! I just could not bring myself to imagine it. I tried to make myself see what I perceived to be the throne room of God. As soon as I relaxed my mind would instantly go someplace else. So I sat there trying, over and over again, to make myself go into the throne room.

After a long time, I found myself able to visualize what I perceived to be the throne room of God. In my minds eye I saw huge wooden doors with gold trim. The shekinah glory of God was shining from within the throne room, but those doors were always shut for me. It was like I could see the throne room, but only from the outside of its closed doors. Underneath those doors, the glory shone through. When I tried to open them, it was like they did not want to open for me. I could not get my mind to open the doors! Amazing!

At that moment, I realized the reason why I could not open the doors and enter in. It was because I did not believe in and see

72

God for who He really is! My concept of Him was still a "God" who was hard to please, and He was not pleased with me. I had always believed that He just put up with me because of Jesus' blood. He tolerated me, but He did not like me. Over a period of time I started to change the way I saw God, I started to see Him as a good God, and a loving Father. I had to lay down my misconception and accept His invitation into the throne room of His glory!

Finally, those doors swung open and the Holy Spirit spoke to me again saying, "Have a look around." To my delight, I saw God on the throne. What did He look like? I have no idea now. However I do remember seeing a great big smile as He stretched out His arms toward me. Everybody in His throne room was looking at me. They were all smiling and very welcoming toward me.

I Experienced His Love!

This was a huge hurdle for me. Once I overcame it, everything about my life changed. From that moment on, my relationship with God changed. Somehow, I had exercised myself to see Him for who He really is rather than who I had always perceived Him to be. It was a major breakthrough!

The Holy Spirit took me through the crowds of people there. I saw and heard all of them affirming and welcoming me. Angels joined in and did the same! People were actually talking to one another saying, "He has finally made it. He has finally believed and come in! He has actually entered in!"

They opened a pathway for me through these thousands and thousands of people as I made my way toward the throne. Father God stood up and put out His hands, taking me upon His lap. He put His arms around me. I was dumbfounded because I had never been able to see that before. This was the first time I had ever been able to experience His love in this way. It was such an awesome love! Wow! I experienced such comfort deep in my heart. I knew that everything was going to be just fine.

From that day forward, my entire Christian life started changing. I began to see things in the Word that I had never seen before. After this experience in the throne room of God, I dared to exercise my mind and my heart to start seeing Him for who He really is. Talk about transformation!

Two Students

A teacher taught a class of primary school students in Seoul, Korea. Of his thirteen pupils, all but two of them happened to really be excelling in his particular class. As a concerned teacher, he was mystified about the situation. He knew very well that these two students had the same capabilities as their classmates. However, the two of them were just not making it. Instead of progressing, they were regressing and seemingly going backwards!

This teacher considered the curriculum, but that was not the reason. He pondered day after day why eleven of his students responded well to him, but the two did not. He felt like he was not being a benefit to these particular kids. They were not learning. They were not passing the tests. He was at a loss as to how to address the situation.

Finally, he received some insight into the nature of the issue. He came up with a plan in which the whole class was given the assignment to draw a picture of their teacher. They were given a piece of paper and a pencil. As the teacher walked around the room monitoring their progress, he noticed a distinct difference between the students who were excelling and the ones who were not. Eleven of the pupils were busy drawing smiling faces, pleasant faces, and funny faces for their teacher. However, the remaining two students were drawing distorted, ugly, mean-looking pictures of their teacher. Then he realized the students' perception of their teacher influenced their ability to perform in the class!

You and I are the same way! Your perception of Father God affects your ability to live the Christian life. Your perception of His character influences the character that is formed in you. I would really like to encourage you to search your heart today. Could it be that your view of God has been distorted?

Change Your Mind

I had to come to that place where I admitted that I was not

seeing God for who He really is. For such a long time, I thought I had my Christian life all together. After being trained for ministry in a Bible school in America, I felt that surely I must have it together! However, things were not all right. I could not know Him very well until that day when I let go of my wrong perceptions and views of Father. I was stuck until that day when I exercised my mind, my heart and my belief system to the place where I could see Him differently. Once I got to the place where I could see Him better, and more the way that the Word portrays Him to be, everything started to change in my life. I'm not fully established yet and I don't think I ever will be because God is so big and infinitely awesome, but dramatic, radical changes began to take place in my life.

I would like to give you examples of these changes, but there were so many! So drastic were the transformations happening within me, that people began to say, "Arthur, do you know how much you have changed?" Then they proceeded to give me specific illustrations of changes they had observed in my life. This happened frequently, even to this day!

The awesome thing is that the changes have occurred effortlessly. Yes, effortlessly! It was not something that I forced to happen out of sheer natural efforts. No! My view of Him changed. My perception of my relationship with Him changed. I repented!

Do you know what the Bible word "repent" means? *"Now after that John was put in prison, Jesus came into Galilee, preaching the gospel of the kingdom of God"* (Mark 1:14) Jesus came and preached the

Good News to the people. He challenged them to "repent" and believe this Gospel. "Repent" means "to change your mind and your thinking." It means "to change what you believe in your heart."

Respond To Him

Father, I worship You today! I am awed by the reality of how easy the Gospel really is. Forgive me for making it so hard and complicated. Thank You for showing me today how my perceptions of You have been distorted. I acknowledge that my views of You have not necessarily been who You really are as my Father.

I ask You to please establish me by Your Spirit and through Your Word in the truth of who You are. Imprint Your true image upon my heart. I want to see You as You really are so that I can be conformed and transformed into Your true image, and not some false image. This is my request today. I receive it by faith! Thank You, Father. Amen.

A Personal Question

May I ask you a personal question while we are in this special place with the Lord right now? Have you found that you have lived your life up until this point with a very distorted picture of who God is? Perhaps the reason for this is because you have never accepted and trusted in the finished work of Jesus for your salvation. I am not talking about raising your hand for a preacher, walking up to the front of a meeting, or even joining a particular church. I mean truly accepting and trusting that the Lord Jesus Christ paid for all of your sin and debt by His blood on the cross and receiving the life that He came to give us when He was raised from the dead.

Have you realized how this message applies to you? Perhaps the reason you have not accepted the life Jesus Christ has so graciously provided for you is because of a wrong concept of who God really is. Hey, if I saw God the way you have (religious, angry, judgmental and demanding), I would not have wanted to have anything to do with Him either! If such a false view has held you back in the past from receiving Him, I want to encourage you to take that step of faith today now that you see the correct view! He loves you very much and wants you to invite Him into your life to stay. He loves you and has forgiven you two thousand years ago, all it takes is for you to accept and receive it as a free gift given to you by God.

Do you want that to change today? Are you saying in your heart right now, "I want to change my wrong concepts, perceptions, and views of God. I want to see and experience God the Father for who He really is. I want my mind to be fixed upon Him so that I can remain in perfect peace." Is this you today?

Pray with me now! Say this out loud to God from your heart...

Father, I come before you in Jesus' name to

worship You. I acknowledge my desire to walk with You. Jesus I confess that You are my Lord and my Saviour. I believe that You loved me so much that you died for me on the cross. Three days later, You were raised again from the dead to live forevermore. Thank You for shedding Your precious blood for me. I now accept and receive your total forgiveness and cleansing of all my sin. Thank You for coming into my heart now and making me Your child. This runaway has now come home to You, my loving heavenly Father.

Congratulations! If you prayed this from your heart today, you can rest assured that your prayer has been answered. Would you please take a moment to contact me at the address or website listed in this book? I want to rejoice with you in what the Lord has done in your life! Praise the mighty name of Jesus! Your experience of the abundant life has just begun!

Eight

Drinking From The Well

W hen I first accepted Jesus as my Lord and Saviour, one of the deepest desires and strongest emotions in my heart was to get to know God intimately. Unfortunately, no one could help me with this when I received the Lord. They were unable to explain how to have a personal relationship with Him. Now, they did tell me about the many different things I needed to do in order to please God. However, they could not assist me with that which was truly most important—getting to know God personally.

I did not necessarily want to be able to memorize and quote all the scriptures I was told I needed to learn. They said, "The way

80

you know God is to read, memorize and confess scripture." At least that is what I heard them say. We do not always hear what people say, but we seem to hear what we think they are saying. Well, whatever the case may be because of what I heard, my attention went from knowing God, to trying to please Him in order to get what He has. My focus changed subtly, but steadily from an intimate relationship with Him to constantly trying to get things out of Him.

Do you see the bait and switch? This was the reason why I did not really get to know God. Although He is our very generous Provider, as a Person He does not allow us to just treat Him mechanically like some celestial vending machine. Intimacy, warmth and closeness were not things I experienced with Him. I was too busy trying to put in the right combination of "coins" and pushing His "button" so that my "stuff" would come out.

For so long in my Christian walk, I mainly only knew about God. I could quote the scriptures and tell you where they were. If pressed, I could even tell you what I thought those scriptures meant, but I was not continually aware of His presence. The only time I would be "aware" of Him (or so I thought) was when I felt really bad for what I did or did not do. Alternating waves of conviction, condemnation and guilt would flood over me for something "bad" I had done or "good" I had left undone. In those times, I concluded that the Holy Spirit was "convicting" me. Thank God today I know better.

The Holy Spirit is not the one who makes you feel guilty, condemned and ashamed! Jesus never made anybody feel guilty, condemned and ashamed. His harshest words were motivated by love toward the hard-hearted, proud religious folks. He was just trying to wake them up! Think about it! Can you point to one place in the New Testament where Jesus looked at a sinner and blasted out, "You filthy, dirty, rotten, scoundrel, scum of the earth. Look at what you are doing!" No! You will not find it even once! If Jesus did not do that, neither will His Spirit! He told us, *"I will send another Comforter to you from the Father"* (John 15:26). The word "another" used here in the original language means "another of the same kind". That means that Jesus was saying that He will send us another of the same kind as He is i.e. the Holy Spirit. The Holy Spirit is just like Jesus, and if Jesus did not condemn people then the Holy Spirit will not condemn people. The Spirit's job is to build up, encourage, and point you to Jesus—not to yourself and your failings all of the time! He wants us to have experiential knowledge of our loving heavenly Father!

Real Love Is Experienced

Christians can talk volumes about the love of God. I remember being able to discuss the love of God at length with anybody long before I had actually experienced it. You see I had an intellectual knowledge about His love, but not an experiential knowledge. What I needed most was to experience His love in reality for myself.

At the time, I could easily say, "God loves you unconditionally, brother. That means He has made a decision to love you. You may not ever experience it with feelings and such, but He loves you." Since experiencing His love personally, I have realized the emptiness of such a statement. Imagine my wife never experiencing my love or my kindness. Lets pretend that she never experiences my love because I do not ever communicate face-to-face, touch, or even really ever spend any time with her. All she gets from me are occasional typed letters from my office delivered by my secretary telling her that I love her and care for her dearly. Finally, one day she tearfully bursts into my room and throws herself at me in complete desperation sobbing, "Arthur, I want to experience you I want to feel this love you say you have for me!"

Imagine me responding coolly and casually, "Well Honey, I have made the decision to love you. Don't you worry about it! All you need to do is believe it", and then I turn around to functionally ignore her again as I get back to the many pressing tasks of my international business!

Will she really ever feel loved? Of course not! Yet that is how you and I often feel God treats us! All we have to do is read the Word and believe that He loves us, but we can never feel or experience it in a personal way. Friend, God's love can be experienced. He is not too busy for you. Your heavenly Father's love is for you to experience today and everyday!

Ugly Idols

Have you ever noticed how mean-looking most idols are that people worship in this world? Stop and observe them sometime. All you have to do is take a glimpse at one of the millions of Hindu gods to see how ugly and mean many of them look. Why is this? Why do men conceive of such "gods" to bow down to and worship? It is because of ignorance and unbelief. The perception that we have of Almighty God since the fall is that He is angry and mean!

If some Christians could project the picture they have in their heart of who they believe God to be, where others could see it, the image would be pretty scary! Certainly, mine was! Looking back, I can now understand why most people did not want to have anything to do with the God I was serving. Truly, the view you have of God influences the quality of every area of your life! Therefore, God will only be real to you to the degree that you have a healthy visual concept of who He truly is.

You may wonder, "But God is invisible. How can I see Him today? Jesus is not standing here in front of me!" Look at Him in the pages of the New Testament. The ink and paper is a spiritual window for you to gaze through to see Him with the eyes of your heart. Jesus plainly told us that if you have seen Him, you have seen Father God. *"Jesus answered: "Don't you know me, Philip, even after I have been among you such a long time? Anyone who has seen me has seen the Father. How can you say, 'Show us the Father'?"* (John 14:9) NIV

Please realize that I am not asking you to see how long His beard was or what color sandals He happened to be wearing. No! His historical physical features are now a moot point. I am talking about seeing what kind of a Person He is! How does He speak and act? What kind of attitudes does He exhibit? How does Jesus treat people? What does He do in certain situations? These are the questions we must seek answers to.

As you see Him for who He really is, you will begin to experience all of the promised benefits of the Christian life. What are these benefits? Some of them include forgiveness of sin, healing, joy, peace of mind, prosperity (wholeness in every part of life including, but not limited to, material provision), strength to endure and the love of God. All of the benefits of the Christian life flow out of the view you have of God. He is your portion. He is your Great Reward. These benefits pour forth directly from His Person into your life as a believer. All His gifts, provisions, and promises are connected to Himself! Therefore, to experience these benefits you must get to know Him for who He really is. Knowing Him is the basis for receiving everything we will ever need for life and godliness! *"Grace and peace be multiplied to you in the knowledge of God and of Jesus our Lord, as His divine power has given to us all things that pertain to life and godliness, through the knowledge of Him who called us by glory and virtue"* (2 Peter 1:2-3) NKJV

Life Giving Water

In the gospel of John chapter four we find Jesus at a well where He met a woman. Jesus did not have anything to draw water out of the well to drink, so He asked the lady, "Draw some water and give Me a drink."

She looked at Him and countered with a question of her own, "You are a Jew. Why do you ask me, a Samaritan woman, to give you something to drink? You Jews have nothing to do with us Samaritans."

In John 4:10 we pick up the story, *"Jesus answered her, "If you knew the gift of God and who it is that asks you for a drink, you would have asked him and he would have given you living water."* NIV

"But Sir, you do not even have anything to draw this water with."

Jesus responded, *"Everyone who drinks this water will be thirsty again, but whoever drinks the water I give him will never thirst. Indeed, the water I give him will become in him a spring of water welling up to eternal life."* (John 4:13-14) NIV

What does this have to do with the view you and I have of God you might ask? Jesus was saying to this woman, "Will you come and drink of the water that I have come to give you? Will you partake of it?" What else did Jesus say when He came? *"I came that they may have and enjoy life, and have it in abundance (to the full, till it overflows)"* (John 10:10) AMP Jesus came to give us something! He came to give us life (Zoe)

Self-Existent

Jesus said, *"If you drink of the water that I have come to give you."* He also declared in John 14, *"If you have seen Me, you have seen the Father."* In John 1:18, John tells us that the purpose for which Jesus came was to reveal who the Father is to the world. *"No man has ever seen God at any time; the only unique Son, or the only begotten God, Who is in the bosom [in the intimate presence] of the Father, He has declared Him [He has revealed Him and brought Him out where He can be seen; He has interpreted Him and He has made Him known]."* AMP

Jesus came to give us a full view of who the Father really is. He told us that if we drink of that water, we would never thirst again. We would never run around trying to get meaning for life from other people or things!

One of the reasons you and I get trapped in sin so easily is because we are not deriving our meaning for life out of our relationship with God. So what do we do? Well, the devil comes and says, "If you only do this you will feel so much better." Just a little more cocaine and you will feel better. One more drink and you will feel better. If you can just get into bed with that other person you will feel so much better. You will feel so good about yourself!" No! That is the lie! The truth is that we will not feel better doing anything apart from knowing and experiencing God. We were created to derive our very life from Him!

In John 4:14 Jesus told the Samaritan woman that this living water would be in her "…a well of water springing up into everlasting life." She had been listening to the devil's lies for many years. Jesus revealed in and through a word of knowledge (verses 16-18) that she had been looking to other empty sources for life. However, Jesus now stood before her offering true life, real life.

In John 5:25-26 (AMP) Jesus reveals the kind of life that He was talking about.

" Believe Me when I assure you, most solemnly I tell you, the time is coming and is here now when the dead shall hear the voice of the Son of God and those who hear it shall live. For even as the Father has life in Himself and is self-existent, so He has given to the Son to have life in Himself and be self-existent."

Notice here that the Amplified bible tells us that this life of God is self-existent. God does not need anybody or anything else outside Notice here that the Amplified bible tells us that this life of God is self-existent. God does not need anybody or anything else outside of Himself in order to have life. He does not derive His life from anything else. Jesus, the Son, has this same self-existent life. This means that when Jesus walked the earth, He did not need anybody else's approval or acceptance to feel good about Himself. He was self-existent. The life of God was in Him. Jesus came to give you and me that very same life! *"I came that they may have and enjoy life, and have it in abundance (to the full, till it overflows)"* (John 10:10) AMP.

There is an important progression of life here. God the Father has life within Him. "Zoe" is the Greek word for the "God-kind of life." He has that life in Him and He is self-existent. He has also given that same self-existent life to the Son, Jesus Christ. Jesus then told us that He came to give us that same kind of self-existent life. God the Father—to Jesus the Son—to you and me His children!

Life Giving

Do not get me wrong! I am not saying that we do not need to rely on God because we have His self-existent life within us now. You must be plugged into the Source of Life by an intimate relationship with Him in order to receive this everlasting, self-existent, God-kind of life. In John 17:3, Jesus makes it very clear when He said, *"And this is life eternal, that they might know thee the only true God, and Jesus Christ, whom thou hast sent." "We live, move, and have our being in Him"* (Acts 17:28). He is in us and we are in Christ. When you have this life bubbling up from Him within you, when you start drinking of the living water Jesus gives you, from the well of your spirit—you will never thirst again! You will never need anything outside of God's life, love and acceptance again.

A couple of years ago a very good friend of mine came to see me, he was very excited, "Arthur!" He exclaimed, "You need to go to these meetings I have been attending. God is moving in a powerful way! This is just what you need." "It was a lifesaver for me," he said, "my life had been so dry and meaningless lately but now I have a new lease on life." We have known each other for many years now, and I realized that he was dead serious about this special meeting at his church. I had attended so many of these special meetings through the years, all of which promised that it would be the answer to what was lacking in my life. Only to find that a couple of days after the meetings when everything was back to normal, the kids were back at school, the phone was ringing at the office, the bills needed paying and the beggar at my door was looking at me for some hand-out there was still a void and a lack in my heart.

But today, as I was listening to Paul's enthusiastic witness, I just did not have the same desire and need to go to yet another special meeting. Although I was sure that these meetings were very good and certainly many people were benefiting from them, I felt a little uncomfortable because I did not know how to tell Paul that I just did not need to go to these meetings. At first I thought that I must be very backslidden and spiritually numb. Guilt and shame started to well up in my heart, because it is generally accepted in Christian circles that if you are a serious and committed Christian (which I considered myself to be) then you should have a continuous desire and need for meetings like these.

Finally I made some excuses for why I would not be able to go with him to the meeting and he went home. I started to think about what had just taken place and I asked the Lord to help me because I did not want to be insensitive to the things of God. I wanted the Lord to show me if there was anything amiss in my relationship with Him. Why is it that I did not have that desire and deep need anymore?

Jesus told the Samaritan woman that this living water would be in her *"...a well of water springing up into everlasting life."* (John 4:14)

Whenever water is mentioned in the word of God it is always a symbol of life. Jesus was making it very clear that there are two sources that we can derive or get life from. Firstly, we can go to all the places or (wells) that this world has to offer. It may be all the places or things that lust, perversion, and the appetites of the flesh have to offer. It may be all the things or places that knowledge and worldly wisdom has to offer, or it might even be all the things or rewards that religion has to offer. But Jesus said, *"Whosoever drinketh of this water shall thirst again:..."* I believe that Jesus is saying that although many of these things or places can give you temporary relief, and even give you some form of life, it cannot satisfy the deep need and thirst in the human heart. Even many of us as Christians go through life drinking at the wells of what this world has to offer. We get involved with religious activities and other so called spiritual things that can only satisfy for short periods. Thus we find Christians running from one place to another, from one meeting to another and from one person to another, looking for that life or significance that only a meaningful, intimate relationship with God can give us.

Secondly Jesus said, *"But whosoever drinketh of the water that I shall give him shall never thirst; but the water that I shall give him shall be in him a well of water springing up into everlasting life."*

91

Jesus is saying, that there is a second eternal source of life, and that source of life is the living water that He has come to give us. If we will drink from this water, or let me put it another way, if we will partake of that which He has come to give us, we will never thirst again. Because within us will spring up a well of life that will sustain us, and we will never have to look anywhere else for significance of life again.

Jesus came to give us Zoe, the life of God, the life that sustains God right now. (John 10:10) That life is a self – existent life that is born out of faith righteousness before God that enables us to have an unbroken, uninterrupted meaningful relationship with God the Father; a relationship where we never have to feel unworthy, unaccepted and unlovable again. This is the meaning of life, this is significance, and this is what every person in the world wants and needs, but this can never be found in any other place, person or thing (well) that this world can offer us.

Unless we start believing fully in the finished work of Jesus we will always thirst. Unless we start to see God for who he really is in and through the wonderful work of Jesus on the cross we will always thirst. The finished work of Jesus on the cross and faith in that work alone is what gives me access to an intimate and personal relationship with Almighty God who is also my Father.

What does this mean to you and I as believers today? If I ever need anything, I can let down and draw some living water from my own everlasting well of intimate fellowship with the father.

Life Is In Him Alone

I have even seen some Christians who think that they need to go to a particular church to have life. They think, "If I do not go to this church, I am not going to have significance in life!" No! Your church is not your true source of life. You do not need your church in that way. Now, it is a good thing to want to have a relationship with your local church. It is not a bad thing to want to be a part of what they are doing. However, you do not need it for your significance. Your local church cannot take the place of God Himself as your Source of life.

Jesus emphatically said that the only place you can get zoe-life is from God Himself. Then, when you partake of it, a spring will well up within you so that you will never thirst again. This means that you will never have to try to derive your life from looking to something or someone else outside of God ever again. Why do people become drug addicts? Why do people become sex addicts? Why do people become alcoholics? Why do people feel they cannot live without something or someone other than God Himself? They are trying to derive meaning for life from these things, instead of from God the Father.

This may sound like a foreign concept to you. We have been taught so often that we need one another, that God has put us together for a reason, that we complement one another, and are more powerful together than only one of us alone. This is true that we are stronger together and complement one another, but we were never meant to derive our meaning for life from anybody else other than God. All of your desire for life can be met through a relationship with God through Jesus Christ. If you have that, then you can truly be complementary to one another. If not, those relationships will just end up being another environment where empty people try to suck life out of each other in various ways.

Personally, I found it sounded a bit strange when I first heard it. I could not understand how I could be self-existent and not need my wife. For a long time I needed my wife in order to feel good about myself. I looked to her for the life I was not finding through an intimate relationship with God. That she is still with me is a miracle from Him in itself! Thank You, Lord! (And thank you, Cathy!) Any time we start to look for life and significance from our spouse we will try to get something from them they cannot give us, and when they are not able to give us what we think we need, we will start looking for someone else that we perceive is able to give us what we need.

Possessing Life Today

Do believers in Jesus have this same self-existent life that the Father and Jesus both have? It is very important that we answer and settle this question in our hearts. In John 10:10, Jesus told us that He came to give us life. 1 John 5:10-13 sheds even more light on this issue.

Verses 10-11 (AMP) begin, *"He who believes in the Son of God [who adheres to, trusts in, and relies on Him] has the testimony [possesses this divine attestation] within himself. He who does not believe God [in this way] has made Him out to be and represented Him as a liar, because he has not believed (put his faith in, adhered to, and relied on) the evidence (the testimony) that God has borne regarding His Son. And this is that testimony (that evidence): God gave us eternal life, and this life is in His Son."*

This passage says those who believe bear within themselves a testimony, or an evidence, which is eternal zoe-life. Notice that it says *"...God gave us..."* past tense. The Bible does not say, "God will give you." You will not have it one day. No, you already have it now! This very minute, you have Zoe-life! Do you know the Son? Have you put your faith and trust in Him for your right standing with God? Yes? Then God's Word says that you have eternal Zoe-life, that same quality of life that the Son has. It is self-existent life. Notice in verse 11; "...this life is in His Son." existent life. Notice in verse 11; *"...this life is in His Son."*

Verse 12 (AMP) continues, *"He who possesses the Son has that life; he who does not possess the Son of God does not have that life."* It is that simple! Do you have the Son? Then you already possess that life. What life? Zoe-life, self-existent life! If you do not have the Son, then you do not have that life. This is not hard to understand!

John continues, *"I write this to you who believe in (adhere to, trust in, and rely on) the name of the Son of God [in the peculiar services and blessings conferred by Him on men], so that you may know [with settled and absolute knowledge] that you [already] have life, yes, eternal life"* (verse 13) AMP

At the risk of sounding redundant, I want to make sure that we are on the same page of understanding concerning this point. God had self-existent life in Himself. He gave it to the Son. Jesus, the Son, gave you and me this same self-existent life. This scripture tells us that John wrote this truth down for us so that we would not be confused, but know that this eternal Zoe-life is already in us.

Nine

Experiencing

Zoe-Life

A s we saw in the previous chapter, the believer has the self existent life of God in him right now. Can anything overcome this life of God? No! Is there anything that can snuff out this life of God? No! Is there any sickness or disease that can stand against this life of God? Of course not! Is there a problem so big and so strong that it could successfully withstand this life of God? No way! Then how come so many of us are struggling?

Did you know that every miracle you are ever going to need in your lifetime is already in you right now? Although this is true, it sounds so foreign to many believers! We have services in which we attempt to "pray down" the blessing of God. We work hard to "pray through" about certain things. "Brother, have you prayed through yet?" is a question we often hear. I always wondered, "Prayed through what?" "Oh, brother we need to press in, we need to press in with God." Just listen to what we are saying. Is God trying to hold us out that we need to press in? The Bible says that if you are born-again, you are in, and resident within you is a well of Zoe-life. If you are thirsty, you can drink of the living water that is already in you. Then how come so many of us are still struggling to experience it when it is clear that we already have it. Why are we not experiencing it? Where is this apparent discrepancy between the truth of the Word and our everyday experience coming from?

Why do we spend most of our time trying to draw a drink from somebody else's well? Certain Christians seem to be special and are somehow able to cause their wells to bubble over in a spectacular way. All of a sudden we have a "move of God" as we call it. There is this superstar preacher who somehow is able to get that living water that is in him out to where other people can drink from it. Then we all choose to just hang around him, drinking from his well and boarding up our own wells.

Choose To Experience Life

Listen to what Paul says to the Christians (Yes, Christians!) who lived at Ephesus. I want you to realize that he was not talking to people in the world. He was talking to true believers!

Ephesians 4:17 (AMP) says, *"So this I say and solemnly testify in [the name of] the Lord [as in His presence], that you must no longer live as the heathen (the Gentiles) do in their perverseness [in the folly, vanity, and emptiness of their souls and the futility] of their minds."*

I used to interpret this scripture out of the legalism that lived in my heart and the way it caused me to see things. When I read the above verse, I heard Paul saying, "You Christians, stop sinning like the rest of the world!" I thought that he was saying, "You must not live like the world! Don't live in sin like the world does!" I want you to notice that Paul was not even talking about sin here. He did not even refer to sin!

Paul was really saying, "Listen, do not walk or choose to live your lives in the same way as the Gentiles. Do not have the same low quality of life that people who do not know God have." This means that Paul was saying, that as born-again believers who have the very self-existent Zoe-life of God within us, our quality of life should at least be better than that of an unbeliever. This verse shows us that it is possible for someone to be a Christian having the very Zoe-life of God within them but not experience or live in it.

Self-Banished

Verse 18 (AMP) continues, *"Their moral understanding is darkened and their reasoning is beclouded. [They are] alienated (estranged, self-banished) from the life of God [with no share in it; this is] because of the ignorance (the want of knowledge and perception, the willful blindness) that is deep-seated in them, due to their hardness of heart [to the insensitiveness of their moral nature]."*

Paul reveals a powerful truth and reality and that is that just like unbelievers are alienated, estranged, and self-banished from the life of God, we as Christians can be just like them. In this process, we must acknowledge the possibility of being a Bible believing, Spirit-filled Christian, but be separated from the very life of God that is in us. You can have it and still not experience it.

Hope deferred makes the heart sick! When you know what the Word of God says you have, but do not experience it, your heart gets sick. One day several years ago my heart got so sick that I finally cursed God. You have to understand that at that stage of my life, things were never my fault. I always had something or somebody else to blame. I must have sounded just like Adam all over again, "No, no, no, God. It was this woman You gave me!" He not only blamed the woman, but also God Himself! We have been the same ever since.

In verse 18, Paul says that just like these unbelievers we are in this place of not experiencing and walking in the fullness of God due to our own ignorance and hardness of heart. This word "hardness" means "callous or insensitive." Before entering the ministry fulltime, I worked with my hands doing various kinds of manual labor. The callouses I used to have on my hands were such that I could literally push a whole needle through them without feeling a thing. The scripture here is saying that you can be a Christian possessing the Zoe-life of God, but because of a lack of perception and the insensitivity of heart, still not experience the benefits of that life. What is this talking about? Well as we have seen in the previous chapters the heart is where we believe. Hardness and insensitivity of heart is when we have unbelief in our hearts. It is when what we believe is "un" or upside down or crooked. In other words we believe but what we believe is incorrect (upside down or crooked). If what we believe is incorrect we are cut off from the very life of God that is within us. The Amplified Bible says it this way in verse 18 *"[They are] alienated (estranged, self-banished) from the life of God [with no share in it]"* Self-banished explains it the way it is. If we are ignorant and cannot see God for who He really is we banish ourselves from the very (Zoe) life of God that is resident in us.

Complete In Him

But look at what Colossians 2:6-10 tell us, *"As ye have therefore received Christ Jesus the Lord, so walk ye in him: rooted and built up in him, and established in the faith, as ye have been taught, abounding therein with thanksgiving. Beware lest any man spoil you through philosophy and vain deceit, after the tradition of men, after the rudiments of the world, and not after Christ. For in him dwelleth all the fullness of the Godhead bodily. And ye are complete in him, which is the head of all principality and power."*(KJV)

101

Notice how he says that in Christ dwells all the fullness of the godhead bodily. Immediately after that statement, he tells us that we are complete in Him. That word "complete" means "lacking or wanting nothing."

Look again at Colossians 2:9-10 in the Amplified Bible; *"For in Him the whole fullness of Deity (the Godhead) continues to dwell in bodily form [giving complete expression of the divine nature]. 10 And you are in Him, made full and having come to fullness of life [in Christ you too are filled with the Godhead--Father, Son and Holy Spirit--and reach full spiritual stature]."*

You are already complete! *"[in Christ you too are filled with the Godhead--Father, Son and Holy Spirit--and reach full spiritual stature].* Who is the "you" being talked about? It is your spirit man. How can we cause something to grow that the Word of God tells us is complete? We cannot! You do not need to add more to something that is not lacking or wanting for nothing. Please understand me correctly. I am not saying that you cannot grow as a Christian. You must grow as a Christian. It is just that your spirit is not the part of you that must grow. It is already complete. You cannot do a thing to influence your spirit-man in any way. You have been absolutely, totally saved. In your spirit-man, you are complete. That is where God's Zoe-life resides in you.

"Well then, what can I change?" I am so glad you asked! Your heart can grow and change. Your belief system needs to mature. The accurate knowledge and perception of who God is, influences the one who knows God. This is the part of you that needs the Word of God, not your spirit-man. Your spirit-man does not need to be fed, but your heart needs input from the Word.

What is your heart? As we have already stated the heart is the part of you where you believe or your belief system. What you believe about God is the pivotal point around which you experience Him. It is because of the insensitivity of your heart or the condition of your belief system, that you can have the very life of God within you, but do not experience it. If you will study the Bible, you will find that you live your entire life out of the heart. Everything you do comes out of what you believe in your heart. Therefore, if what you believe about God, yourself, and others around you does not line up with the truth, then you cannot experience the truth!

Crooked Or Straight?

Proverbs 17:20 says, *"He that hath a froward heart findeth no good."* The word "froward" means "crooked, bent, or out of shape." By way of contrast, the root word for "righteous" and "righteousness" means "straight." Righteousness and truth are straight. If your heart is bent or crooked, it will not be able to allow the straight truth of the Zoe-life that is within you to flow through. Your heart is like a channel for the living water within. When what you believe is not based on truth, it blocks up the channel. When your belief system is crooked and bent out of shape, the living waters of the Zoe-life of God that is inside cannot get to the outside where it is experienced.

I used to understand the word "unbelief" to only mean "the inability to believe something." Now I can see that "unbelief" is more than just that. "Unbelief" is a very active word. As I have said previously, unbelief is when you believe from your heart in such a way that what you "believe" is "un". This is when what you "believe" is turned inside out and upside down or incorrect. Therefore, unbelief is when you want to and try to "believe," but your heart truly believes something else. The belief system of the heart always overrides what the conscious mind can only agree to and accept what it believes is truth.

Every Christian believes in God. However, when you believe incorrectly about Him from your heart, you will not experience Him for who He really is. This is why it is imperative that every believer know Him as the loving Father He really is. This will enable you to experience Him. When your heart is upright and straight according to truth, then you will be able to experience the awesome God who lives inside of you. I used to think that an "upright heart" was talking about a sinless person who was just, holy and perfect. Now I know that the Bible is really talking about someone whose belief system is upright. It is not filled with unbelief. Your heart is straight and serves as an open channel to the living waters resident within to flow out from your inner being to your life experience.

Look at Proverbs 17:20 again. *"He that hath a froward heart findeth no good."* The person who has a deceitful and crooked heart cannot find good. The individual whose belief system is crooked cannot find any good. The Word does not say that good is absent, only that this person cannot find it. In fact, they might actually be surrounded by good, but because of the crookedness of their heart they will only see the negative and will totally miss the positive.

Straighten out the way you believe in your heart with the Word of God, and you will find that Zoe-life is set free to flow from within you. I know it is frustrating to live in chaos and confusion when we know the Bible says that Zoe-life is the quality of life we have been given by God. God does not want us to stay this way! If you do not get to know the Father for who He really is from your heart, then the life that is in you will be functionally out of reach. Christianity is all about believing right, or persuading our hearts. The only effort in Christian life is in the believing, not in the doing. Put the same effort into persuading and changing what you believe, that you have put into trying to live right and do right, and see what power will be released in your life.

Recovery of Sight

"The Spirit of the LORD is upon Me, Because He has anointed Me To preach the gospel to the poor; He has sent Me to heal the brokenhearted, To proclaim liberty to the captives and recovery of sight to the blind, To set at liberty those who are oppressed" (Luke 4:18) NKJV

In this passage in Luke, Jesus states that He has come for the *"recovery of sight"* to the blind. This does not necessarily mean the physical healing of blind eyes. But I believe it is talking about the recovering of our awareness of who God is and seeing Him as He really is. It is the same phrase in the Greek as in John 17:1 where Jesus *"lifted up His eyes"*.

"Jesus spoke these words, lifted up His eyes to heaven, and said: "Father, the hour has come. Glorify Your Son, that Your Son also may glorify You, as You have given Him authority over all flesh, that He should give eternal life to as many as You have given Him. And this is eternal life, that they may know You, the only true God, and Jesus Christ whom You have sent."(John 17:1-4) NKJV

Notice, *"He lifted up His eyes to heaven and said, Father…"*. Jesus recovered His sight! Pay special attention to how Jesus addressed God. He did not go, "O, God!" He just remembered who His Father is and recovered His awareness of this fact. Part of experiencing God is the constant awareness of Him as your Father. Jesus reminded Himself of who God is, and said, "Father". Just as Jesus needed to recover sight, you and I need to recover our sight. We need to start seeing things for what they really are!

"Father, the hour has come. Glorify and exalt and honor and magnify Your Son, so that Your Son may glorify and extol and honor and magnify You," (John 17:1)AMP Jesus made a very valid point here. He said, "Father, glorify Me." "Glorify" literally speaks of the view and opinion of God, which is reality. Jesus was saying, "God, glorify Me. Show Me again who I am. Let Me know who I am so that I may glorify You." One of the reasons why Christians find it hard to worship God is because we do not believe who He says we are!

Verse 2 (AMP) continues, *"[Just as] You have granted Him power and authority over all flesh (all humankind), [now glorify Him] so that He may give eternal life to all whom You have given Him."* Who are all that have been given to Jesus? Everyone! (See John 3:16) For this reason Jesus declares here in John 17: 3, *"And this is eternal life: [it means] to know (to perceive, recognize, become acquainted with, and understand) You, the only true and real God, and [likewise] to know Him, Jesus [as the] Christ (the Anointed One, the Messiah), Whom You have sent."* Jesus was saying "God, show Me, help Me, let Me see who I am. Remind Me. I am recovering My sight so that I can glorify You. I am recovering My sight so that I can take this Zoe-life You have given Me and give it to the world."

The Only True and Real God

What is this eternal life? Jesus says, eternal life is knowing, perceiving, recognizing, becoming better acquainted with and understanding that the Father is the only true and real God! Jesus was saying that the only way you can have and experience the self-existent, divinely given Zoe-life is by coming to know the true and real God and His Son. Either way, knowing the Father and knowing Jesus is the same deal. So it basically boils down to this: what you believe about God in your heart will affect the experience you have as a Christian. Your belief system affects your experience of God.

In my Christian life, I could never understand how the Word could have so many wonderful promises for me, but I could never seem to experience them. I thought that I just did not have the right formula, or I did not have the faith needed to make it all work. So I would run to as many meetings and preachers as I could, begging "Give me another formula!" I see this same problem in many others today who come up to me after I speak asking, "What must I do?" Let me explain something to you. It is nothing you can do! The right question centers on, "What are you believing in your heart?"

The abundant Christian life and experiencing God are all about what you believe. It is not about what you are doing. What do you believe in your heart? What do you believe about God? Do you really know Him? Do you really know who He is? His Word says that if you do, you will start to experience life!

As you continue to process in your mind and in your heart these truths that you are reading about, it is good for you to keep going back to the Lord every few steps along the way. Even if these things stay with you in your intellect, they will not do you much good until they penetrate your heart. Until they impact your personal, intimate relationship with Him, your experience will not really change. In fact, the information in this book could potentially leave you more frustrated than ever before!

Therefore, I highly encourage you to really pray these prayers from your heart. They are included to spur you on toward taking this information into your heart where the Holy Spirit

Himself will ignite it into revelation to you. Use these prayers as a spiritual springboard into His presence where He is waiting with love to meet with you. There, you will experience Him. The result will be true transformation.

Glory To Glory

Let us pray: Father, I come before You to worship and honor You. Thank You for showing me that my Christian life is what I believe, in Whom I believe. I want to know You intimately, more intimately than ever before! I want the real and true knowledge of You to permanently affect me deep within.

Thank You, Father, for giving me Your Zoe-life. I acknowledge that I truly have eternal life. I am being transformed and changed from glory to glory as I get to know You better. I find myself falling more in love with You today than ever before! Hallelujah! Thank You that life becomes easier and gets better each day I fall deeper in love with You! You give me strength to face the challenges that come my way.

Father, I am recognizing now, more than ever before, all of the belief structures within my heart that are really just unbelief. The reason that I am not experiencing You and Your Zoe-life manifest in my life more than I do is because of the way I have believed. It is

not because You are holding something back from me. It is not because You do not want me to have it. You really do love me! You have already provided! You do want me to have it!

Establish me in the true and correct knowledge of You so that my heart will be so influenced that I will never be the same again! I want to live my life truly and regularly experiencing You from this day forward. Amen!

Ten

Abba-Father

G od is the Almighty One but He is also our Father! The world does not see Him as Father. Religious people cannot perceive Him as Father. When you get to know Him as Father, and then try to tell others about Him, the religious will want to silence you. How do I know that you may ask? This was the religious people's response to Jesus. When He told them of the Father, they wanted to kill Him.

The Vision

Many years ago, I was meditating upon the Word of God in Matthew 27. This chapter details the events surrounding the crucifixion. I remember verses 50-51 grabbing my attention: *"Jesus, when he had cried again with a loud voice, yielded up the ghost. And, behold, the veil of the temple was rent in twain from the top to the bottom; and the earth did quake, and the rocks rent."*

All of a sudden, I had a vision. I saw thousands of people around the feet of Jesus. They were worshiping Him, trying to touch Him and be with Him. The whole picture seemed strange to me. Jesus stood on a stage-like structure above them. The people could almost reach His feet. Thousands upon thousands pushed and pulled one another trying to get near Him. The scene reminded me of a huge rock concert in some ways. People were practically climbing over the top of others in order to get to Him. The part that seemed strange was the fact that Jesus, standing above them on this stage-like structure kept saying, "Shoo! Shoo! Go away!"

I thought that to be very strange, so I asked, "Lord, why are You chasing the people away?" In my mind, the people were right to throng Him in this manner. They were worshiping Him, desiring to be with Him, and recognizing Him as their Lord and Saviour! Yet He kept going, "Shoo! Shoo! Go away!" For a long time I saw this picture without understanding. When I had read the scripture over once again, the Lord spoke something to my heart that has changed my understanding forever: He said, "I came to make the way clear for you to have a one-on-one personal relationship with the Father, but you are still hanging around My feet."

In that one explosive statement, Jesus effectively dynamited many of my established theological assumptions. He blew me right out of the water of my religiosity, because the content of that statement did not fit within the framework of my view of God back then. You see, for all of my Christian life Jesus was the only One I could approach. He was the "Nice Guy." He had shed His blood for the forgiveness of my sins. I viewed God as "The God-Father." Just like the patriarchal leader of a feared mafia family in New York City. I heard God speak to me in a husky voice with an unmistakably thick Italian accent, "I make-a you-an offer that-a you cannot-a refuse. You-a give-a your tithe, or I kill-a you! I will not like to-a do it, but I-a have to!" This is maybe a little light hearted, but in effect that is how many believers view God. I have good news for you today! God is not in a bad mood. He is not one step away from zapping you off the planet. Yet, many Christians persist in looking at God through these anxious, fear-filled eyes.

Matthew 27 and verse 51 states that the veil in the temple between the holy place and the holy of holies was torn in two from top to bottom upon Jesus' death. You see, at that very moment the sacrifice for sin had been made. Father God was so eager to enjoy restored fellowship with mankind that He did not even wait for the resurrection to tear the veil. That ought to tell you something!

The veil was a thick, heavy, purple curtain that only the high priest could go behind once a year. So fearful was this place called the Holy of Holies that the high priest wore bells on his clothes and a rope around his ankles to do the annual job. The helpers waiting outside listened intently for the steady tinkling of the bells. They stood ready to pull the corpse of the high priest out should he do something to offend God and fall over dead. This was the veil that was torn in two by God Himself! It stood almost two stories high. From top to bottom it was rent. No man could have done that, only God Himself! Hallelujah!

When Jesus died, all that was necessary to provide for our acceptance into the presence of God was forever satisfied. God spoke to my heart in this vision saying, "Now you can come to Me and have a relationship with Me." Immediately, something changed within me and the fear left. I experienced an overwhelming desire to get to know who God my Father is.

Now does that mean that we are to ignore Jesus? No my friend, Jesus is our Lord and eternal Saviour and forever we will be in fellowship and relationship with Him, but His whole purpose was to restore our fellowship with the Father.

Attracted To Him

Everybody quotes John 3:16, *"For God so loved the world..."* The way I used to hear and understand that verse was "God so loved the world that He felt obligated to do something for you." No! That is not it! He so LOVED you that out of this LOVE He

114

made it possible for you to approach Him through the veil, which was the physical body of Jesus Christ. You can now enter in and have an intimate relationship with Father God.

I had never experienced that before! Sure, I worshiped Jesus and could talk to Him, but something changed! No longer was God Almighty like a mafia patriarch to me. His voice changed (at least my perception of it did!), and so did mine. No longer did I feel I had to pray at the top of my lungs in religious King James Authorized old English saying, "Dear GGGAAAWWWDDD!" Because my view and opinion of Him had changed, I started wanting to get close to Him. When I began to see Him for who He really is, I found myself being irresistibly drawn to Him. He is so attractive!

People have asked me the question, "Why do you think the power of God is not currently working in the Church in the same way that it was in the book of Acts?" I believe that one of the reasons for this is the "God" we see and serve is not the God of the Bible. I hope you understand what I mean. Our view of Him is incorrect. God only manifests His power as a confirmation that His message is being preached. He does it to acknowledge an accurate representation of His character. It is His seal of approval on the Word being given. I believe He is saying to many people in the Body today, "I am not going to confirm that 'word' you are giving because I am not like what you are talking about. That is not who I am and I do not want My people confused. Therefore, declare who I really am and then watch Me confirm with power, signs, and wonders!"

When people are confronted with a message like the one in this book, many respond by getting mad, angry and offended because they have already established their "Christian life" and in effect have built their theology and view of God as a little, comfortable house. They say, "We have already built it the way we want it!" Then, somebody like me comes along challenging them, "To have another look at things." All of a sudden they get mad because the mansion I am describing does not resemble the shack they had considered a "palace." Most people's little Christian house as it were, is coming apart and cracking up. The problem is that you cannot just continue patching up and hiding the flaws you have in your theology if your foundation is wrong. Jesus came to show you the view that He had of God the Father. Even if it is totally different from yours, humble yourself and move on into the mansion. "Repent and believe this Gospel…! Shack or mansion, it is your choice!

Freaking Out!

There is such power in knowing and experiencing God for who He really is. Knowing and experiencing God as our loving Father brings tremendous peace and emotional stability into effect. No adverse circumstance no matter how big or dark, will be able to shake or disturb that peace.

Then they went to a place called Gethsemane, and He said to His disciples, Sit down here while I pray. And He took with Him Peter and James

116

and John, and began to be struck with terror and amazement and deeply troubled and depressed. And He said to them, My soul is exceedingly sad (overwhelmed with grief) so that it almost kills Me! Remain here and keep awake and be watching. And going a little farther, He fell on the ground and kept praying that if it were possible the [fatal] hour might pass from Him. And He was saying, Abba, [which means] Father, everything is possible for You. Take away this cup from Me; yet not what I will, but what You [will]. (Mark 14:32-36) AMP

Jesus experienced the darkest hour of His life in the Garden of Gethsemane. He already knew He was going to die on a cross within a short time. Jesus was aware of the physical, mental, and emotional pain that He was about to suffer. (Mark 14:32-33) AMP relates, *"Then they went to a place called Gethsemane, and He said to His disciples, Sit down here while I pray. And He took with Him Peter and James and John..."* These guys were His closest buddies. They were the ones who had boldly declared, "Jesus, even if we have to die with You, we are going to be with You!" Jesus understood that they were not able to do so. He knew that they were going to despise and abandon Him. Jesus foresaw Peter turning around soon and declaring, "I do not know this man!" He knew these things there in the garden of Gethsemane!

"...and began to be struck with terror and amazement and deeply troubled and depressed" (Mark 14:33) AMP. Now I want you to notice that Jesus was struck with terror! One time I was preaching this and a lady in the audience sat there going "What?" After the service she told me, "I never thought that Jesus ever could have been afraid!" Many of us were taught that Jesus could not be afraid

because He was the Son of God. After all He is God! You have to understand something—Jesus was also 100% man, like you and me. *"Let this same attitude and purpose and [humble] mind be in you which was in Christ Jesus: [Let Him be your example in humility:] Who, although being essentially one with God and in the form of God [possessing the fullness of the attributes which make God God], did not think this equality with God was a thing to be eagerly grasped or retained, But stripped Himself [of all privileges and rightful dignity], so as to assume the guise of a servant (slave), in that He became like men and was born a human being. And after He had appeared in human form, He abased and humbled Himself [still further] and carried His obedience to the extreme of death, even the death of the cross!"* (Philippians 2:5-8) AMP

Not only was He struck with terror, but also amazement. He was entering the unknown. Jesus was deeply troubled and depressed about doing something difficult that He had never done before. *"And He said to them, My soul is exceedingly sad (overwhelmed with grief) so that it almost kills Me! Remain here and keep awake and be watching"* (Mark 14:34). Jesus was not just a little perplexed about what was about to happen to Him, He was freaking out!

If that were me I would have been thinking, "Get me a way out!" This scripture describes Jesus as being more than just a little bit apprehensive. The humanity of Jesus Christ was crying out. His flesh was freaking out. Personally, I would have been totally irrational. If some one would have come up to me while I was in such a state saying, "Arthur, I have a problem, or a need. I would have screamed, "Listen, pal! I do not want to know your problems right now. You do not know what I am going through!"

118

But Jesus had a view of God that enabled Him to have a rest and peace in times of great distress and extreme trouble that nobody else could have had. His view and relationship with His Father sustained and stabilized Him. Verse 35, (AMP) continues, *"And going a little farther, He fell on the ground and kept praying that if it were possible the [fatal] hour might pass from Him."* If it were possible? If that were me, I would have demanded, "Make it possible! You are Almighty God and I want out!"

Secure in Father's Pleasure

But Jesus asked, "If it is possible for this hour to pass from me." Notice, He was still rational, even while freaking out and being perplexed and overwhelmed. Then He said, *"Abba, [which means] Father, everything is possible for You. Take away this cup from Me; yet not what I will, but what You [will]"* verse 36,(AMP). Did you see that? He said "Abba-Father." Look at the change in Him. What follows, is the most selfless statement anybody could ever have made. In effect Jesus was saying, "You could stop this whole thing if I asked You to because nothing is impossible for You. Nevertheless, not My will, but Yours be done." Only a man who knows His Father God could have said that and meant it.

Jesus in the darkest hour of His life, with that innate human sense of self-preservation running high until the very moment He addressed His Father "Abba", in doing so remembers who He is, who his Father is and experiences a calm and peace that washes over His anguished soul. As that peace flooded His troubled heart,

Jesus was able to say those now famous words, " Not My will, but Yours be done."

Christ's view of God gave Him such an emotional stability, and divine peace, that it did not matter what crossed His path at that moment. He saw and related to God as His Abba-Father, who said, Mark 1:11, *"... Thou art my beloved Son, in whom I am well pleased."* (KJV)

Jesus knew and understood God His Father to be a loving, forgiving, and caring Father. He knew that He did not have to perform in order for Abba to be happy with Him. Jesus was freaking out in His humanness until He reminded Himself of His Father's words of love. Jesus knew His Father's pleasure. He confidently knew and believed that His relationship was safe and secure.

This was the revelation that separated Jesus from the rest of the religious people of His day. He had this view firmly established in His heart. This reality served as the bedrock of His belief system. He had both the knowledge and the experience of His Father's love and pleasure. This view made Jesus different from all of the other preachers of His day. There were many traveling and resident religious teachers at that time. Some of them were probably more eloquent speakers than He was. Some of them were probably more scholarly than Him. However, Jesus Christ had a view, an opinion, and a belief system that was based on knowing God as His Abba Father. This knowledge separated Him from all the rest!

Set Apart

As Christians, you and I should be separated from both the unbelieving and the religious worlds because of this intimate knowledge of God as our Abba-Father too! Our view and opinion of God should bring us deep heart peace in times of instability and pain. Our personal experience of His love should calm us as we affirm and acknowledge our secure relationship with Him. When there is chaos and distress all around, the life and peace of God should flow freely from within giving us rock solid stability to go on. God's rest is the very trait should set us apart.

We see that Jesus had a view of God the Father that enabled Him to have a supernaturally high degree of emotional stability right there in the midst of His deepest and darkest hour. Everything in Christ's life was coming apart, except Him.

Have you ever been in what seemed to be the deepest and darkest time of your life? Have you ever experienced everything coming apart, even in spite of all of your "believing?" Are you in such a place right now? Jesus knows! He has been there before and He is with you now.

Therefore, since we have a great high priest who has gone through the heavens, Jesus the Son of God, let us hold firmly to the faith we profess. For we do not have a high priest who is unable to sympathize with our weaknesses, but we have one who has been tempted in every way, just as we are-yet was without sin. Let us then approach the throne of grace with confidence, so that we may receive mercy and find grace to help us in our time of need. (Hebrews 4:14-16)NIV

In Gethsemane, Jesus could be rational and selfless. His world was disintegrating on the outside, but inside there was peace. Jesus could do what no other man could do back then because of the way He viewed God. A healthy visual image of Abba-Father sustained Him and gave Him this inner stability and rest. This same peace is available to you and me today as we understand and believe our right standing with Abba-Father!

Eleven

Righteous!

herefore, since we are justified (acquitted, declared righteous, and given a right standing with God) through faith, let us [grasp the fact that we] have [the peace of reconciliation to hold and to enjoy] peace with God through our Lord Jesus Christ (the Messiah, the Anointed One). Through Him also we have [our] access (entrance, introduction) by faith into this grace (state of God's favor) in which we [firmly and safely] stand. And let us rejoice and exult in our hope of experiencing and enjoying the glory of God" (Romans 5:1-2)AMP

Look at the beginning of those verses again. Consider the word "justified." It is the same word translated "righteous" or "righteousness" in most other places. I like to explain the word "justified" like this: "just-as-if-I-have-never-sinned." This is actually all that word is saying. Therefore, since we are "just-as-if-I-have-never-sinned" by faith, it means that right now you are in the presence of God as if you had never sinned. Sin no longer hinders you from entering and abiding in Abba-Father's presence, because He has declared you righteous. By personal faith in Jesus, you have been forever acquitted in God's sight from the judgment your old sin nature deserved and the separation from God that came with it. At the very moment you received Jesus by faith, you were given Christ's eternally righteous nature. You were ushered into His presence with a divinely bestowed right to stand before God, your Abba-Father!

You must learn to recognize and understand that righteousness is not a law for you to obey. It is not even a standard of moral conduct that you must live up to. These are common misconceptions of righteousness carried over from an Old Covenant "works" mentality. Righteousness and justification in the New Testament are words referring to the position you have as a believer in the presence of God. As a bona fide child of God, you may approach His throne any time you want by nature of your family relationship. This position is not based upon your performance. You entered it by faith in the perfect performance of Jesus. You walk in it continually by faith in the finished work of Christ. Therefore, righteousness and justification are not things you must do in order to get, or even to keep, access to God your Father. They are yours by faith in Christ alone!

So if we read the first part of Romans 5 with this understanding, it reads, "Now that you are just-as-if-you-have never-sinned by faith, you "have peace." Peace can only enter into your life if you truly believe by faith that you are just-as-if-you have-never-sinned. Most people talk about peace as if it is a commodity to be had. "Give me some peace, Lord!" We tend to think that God is going to take out a container in which He stores peace and give us each a little dab. You need to know that the way you get THE PEACE OF GOD is to be AT PEACE WITH GOD! It comes as a by-product of faith righteousness because by faith you are just-as-if-you-have-never-sinned. As soon as you accept the Lord Jesus Christ as your Savior, as far as God the Father is concerned you are just-as-if-you-have-never-sinned.

Your Adamic Sin Nature

For some perspective on all of this, may I backtrack a little bit? In the Old Covenant, God demanded perfection. He started with Abram in Genesis 17:1 telling him, "I am going to make a covenant with you. All you have to do, Abram, is be perfect." At the ripe old age of 99, Abram fell flat on his face when he heard this requirement.

I find it interesting that God never said this to Abram when he was sixteen years old, full of youthful idealism and inexperience. God is the Eternal One. He could have chosen to approach Abram at any time in his life. However, God picked this time. At 99 years old, Abram was on the threshold of having a century worth of life experience behind him. He had lived his life! This is when God came to him and said, "I am going to make a covenant with you now. Everything I have is going to be yours. Everything you have is going to be Mine. All I require of you is to be perfect before Me." Abram immediately fell flat on his face. Why? He knew he could not do it! God knew it too, yet He still wanted to cut covenant with this man.

Under the Old Covenant, even if someone could keep all of the law, they would still be a sinner and go to hell. You were a sinner by nature. You were a sinner by what Adam did and passed on to you, not by what actions or inactions you committed. This is what it meant to be a sinner by nature. It is who you were! You were a sinner, but not because you could not keep the law perfectly. God gave His people the law to help them recognize the fact of their sin nature. It was not because they committed sinful acts personally and individually that they were condemned. Adam sinned and all of mankind after him was born with a sin nature (See Romans 5:12-21). This was the real reason all of the people under the Old Covenant were headed for hell apart from Christ!

You say, "Well, that is unfair! People should be judged on their own merit apart from Adam." First, nobody said that the Gospel is fair. In fact, the Gospel is not about fairness at all! The centerpiece of the Bible's narrative is not God's justice. Do not misunderstand me. Of course He is just. Yes, He is the Judge. But this enters into the picture along the way. It is not the main attraction. The central focus is God the Father so desiring to extend mercy to fallen man, that He sacrifices Himself in His own

Son to provide a way to do so. The centerpiece of the Word of God is the Father, Son and Holy Spirit saying together, "We love you so much that we are going to do something about it." This is the main message of the Bible! It is all about the love of a Father for His children, saying, "I will do whatever it takes to reconcile the world to Myself."

Man got into the mess of sin through Adam, but God got man out of the mess of sin by Jesus Christ, the Last Adam. Man received a sin nature through Adam. But God gave man a new righteous nature two thousand years ago through Jesus Christ, the Last Adam. Praise God! No, it is not fair - it is mercy! Mercy triumphs over judgment. God's nature longs to extend mercy. Our part is to receive His mercy by faith in the finished work of Jesus.

Your Righteous Christ Nature

I am trusting that the Holy Spirit is giving you revelation of what I am sharing with you right now. The world was not going to hell because of what they did, or what they were doing. It was not their actions of sin that condemned them to hell. The problem was their sin that they got from Adam. Similarly now, as a believer you are not going to heaven because of what you did, are doing, or are going to do. It is not your actions and/or inactions of right conduct that open heaven's door to you. Your new nature of righteousness does so. This new nature was made available to you in and through the finished work of Jesus on the cross. You are just-as-if-you-have never-sinned because of what Jesus did. Righteous is who you are right now (Romans 5:17; 2 Corinthians 5:21). Now, you received all of this by faith! (You probably need to re-read these last few paragraphs over again slowly so that the meaning can really sink in. This is very offensive to the religious mindsets!)

So you see, our performance is completely out of the way. You and I are just as-if-we-have-never-sinned because of the performance of Jesus. We are accepted in the very presence of God our Father not because of the way we live, or our moral conduct, or how much religious activity we do (including reading the Word, preaching around the world, or praying and fasting—although these things are good in their place). You and I are accepted only because of what Jesus did! It is the only thing we can rely on for our righteousness and right standing before the Father.

Right about this time, most people's minds ask, "Does this mean I can live in sin and get away with it?" No! Sin will kill you. The bible says, Roman 6:23 *"For the wages of sin is death,..."* (NIV) Notice that the word does not say that God will kill you when you sin, but instead it says that "sin" will kill you. You see, sin itself will bring death to your life. It will kill your relationships, it will kill your friendships and ultimately it will kill you physically. Besides, why would you want to invite death when you have been given eternal Zoe-life? Why would you want to cut yourself off from experiencing the love of your Father for a fleeting moment of deceptive enjoyment? Who, in their right mind, would willingly forfeit the experience of living in the awareness of their Father's manifest presence and pleasure? No one I know of, and besides, sin will kill you!

Romans 5:2 (AMP) says again, *"Through Him also we have [our] access (entrance, introduction) by faith into this grace (state of God's favor) in which we [firmly and safely] stand. And let us rejoice and exult in our hope of experiencing and enjoying the glory of God."* Ours is a relationship of grace. Ephesians 2:8 tells us that we entered that relationship by grace through faith. It is through the work of Jesus that you and I are just-as-if-we-have-never-sinned. This relationship does not start with grace and end with works. God is both Author and Finisher! He finishes our relationship by grace through faith as well. It starts and ends with grace and faith. Therefore, you and I stand before God our Father today totally accepted. There is absolutely no reason why He will not do what His Word says He will do for us In order for God not to do what He said he would do, Jesus has to fail. Impossible!

Grasping the Fact

Stay with me here, this is such an awesome progression. We have access by faith into this grace in which we stand. *"And let us rejoice and exult in our hope of experiencing and enjoying the glory of God"* (Romans 5:2) AMP "Hope" means "having a confident expectation of good things." Follow with me in the progression.

Because you are just-as-if-you-have-never-sinned (righteous) by faith in Jesus, you have peace with God (as a by-product of recognizing your right standing with Him). Only when you have this peace with God can you stand in a relationship with Him of grace (not trying to perform to earn it). It is at this point that we can have hope. It is in this place of knowing Him that we will have a confident expectation of good things. What good things? Enjoying and experiencing the glory of God. This means enjoying and experiencing Him in all of His goodness. I pray that you are seeing this. This will revolutionize your Christian life!

"Moreover [let us also be full of joy now!] let us exult and triumph in our troubles and rejoice in our sufferings, knowing that pressure and affliction and hardship produce patient and unswerving endurance" (Romans 5:3) AMP. This verse in the KJV says, *"And not only so, but we glory in tribulations also: knowing that tribulation worketh patience."* That last phrase "worketh patience" can also be rendered "produces perseverance."

"And endurance (fortitude) develops maturity of character (approved faith and tried integrity). And character [of this sort] produces [the habit of] joyful and confident hope of eternal salvation. Such hope never disappoints or deludes or shames us, for God's love has been poured out in our hearts through the Holy Spirit Who has been given to us," (Romans 5:4-5) AMP

Based on a casual reading of this passage of scripture in Romans 5:5, we usually tend to think that all these qualities listed will automatically show up and make themselves available to us during a time of tribulation. Therefore we feel that when we go through tribulations, trials and temptations that it is the very tribulations, trials and temptations that will produce patience, longsuffering and maturity of character. But, let us go over the progression again: We are righteous, just-as-if-we-have-never sinned. Because of this, we are in a state of peace in our relationship with God (no longer enemies, we are on the same side).

It is at this point that the Word says, *"...let us [grasp the fact.."* (Romans 5:1) AMP. Consciously and actively grasp a hold of the fact that you are righteous. Everything between you and God is all right. Consciously and actively grasp a hold of the fact that there is peace between you and God. You have been given a new nature of righteousness by faith and you walk in relationship with Him by grace. You have a confident expectation (hope) of good things coming your way. This is that which you are to grasp. "Grasp" in the Greek is the picture of a man grasping hold of a life preserver when he is drowning. Grab a hold of these things as if your life depends on it! Because these very things will work in you patience in a time of tribulation, these very things will work in you endurance and a mature character, which in turn will give you hope for your future, a hope that will never disappoint you.

Confident Expectation of Good

When you understand your relationship with the Father, and you know Him intimately as Father, then you will grasp a hold of those truths. In the midst of trying times, you will have the inner strength to persevere!

Friend, when you know who God is and when you know who you are in Christ, you can get through anything that comes your way. If you do not know who God is, then you will have quite a time in the midst of turmoil! Understand the righteous nature that you have received, by faith in the finished work of Jesus Christ. Believe your right standing with Him. Comprehend the peace you have with God. Walk in this loving relationship by the grace He has provided from start to finish. You are more than a conqueror in Him! You can get through anything because God's glorious goodness is coming your way!

Twelve

Divine Purpose

Have you ever noticed that Jesus did not just say, "Father," but rather "Abba-Father?" The Hebrew word for "Abba-father" is an affectionate term for addressing your father. It is almost like "daddy," but "Abba" is not something a little child would call his father. "Abba" is a term of endearment used by a more mature child, not by a toddler. This word expresses the love and confidence of a mature child who knows who his father is, his father's status, his father's power, his father's character; and because they know these things they call him "Abba-father." In the Jewish culture of that day, this usually happened at or after their coming of age. Bar-mitzvahs and bat-mitzvahs celebrate when a child turns either thirteen or

133

fourteen years of age. They have entered into the age of accountability and are becoming increasingly more responsible for themselves, including their own sin. Only then, or thereafter, would a child call their father "Abba."

As you know very well by now, for a significant portion of my Christian life I struggled to see God for who He really is. I viewed God as my "Master." He had to accept me because Jesus had shed His blood on my behalf. However, I believed God Almighty did not like me. I believed that He just tolerated me. Every time I made a mistake, it seemed that God Almighty angrily yelled, "I am going to kill you!" and at that time it took Jesus fervently interceding for me, "The Blood! The Blood, Father," that kept me from getting zapped. God was like, "Oh, I almost forgot!" as He stayed His hand of execution one more time. Praise God! That has changed.

Finally, I found out that I was wrong! Abba-Father actually loves and cares for us deeply. Yet for as long as I saw Him as my "Master," I could not experience Him any other way. I have found that many Christians still live trapped in a Master-slave mentality.

A Vertical Relationship?

In the mind of a Hebrew slave, the word "master" had a certain meaning. Even though the servant knew the master, knew his power, knew his character and who his master was, that slave or servant could never affectionately call him "Abba." Only a son or daughter could do that! That slave or servant had to call him "master." This word for "master" in the Greek comes from a combination of two other words. The first meaning "to be the pilot or the steer man of a ship." In reference to authority, it means, "to be the governor or the guide, to be lord." Is Jesus our Lord? Yes, but He does not act toward us in the manner of a slave-driving master. The second Greek word means "to exercise lordship, or to be down upon."

I always saw God as the Lord who was down upon me every time I made a mistake. "Slave, you made a mistake." Slap, slap! He was down upon me. Every time I even merely thought about doing something out of His will, I believed He sent the "Hound of Heaven" down upon me. Who is that you might ask? The Holy Spirit, of course! I saw Him chasing me down, hunting me down, as a predator seeking his prey. I viewed Him as a "down upon" God.

Jesus did not see God this way. He viewed God as His Abba- Father, not as His "Master." Their relationship was not that of a "Master" and "Slave," but as a "Father" and "Son." Christ was loved by and equal to the Father. (This usually ruffles some feathers when I start to explain it.) The view that Jesus had of His relationship with His Father was that He (the Son) was equal to and loved by the Father. Religious folks hated that saying, "How dare you call God your Father and make yourself equal to God!" Hey, it was all true!

Have you ever referred to your relationship with God as a "vertical relationship?" We like to contrast this "vertical relationship" with what we call our "horizontal relationships," meaning the other people around us. Are you familiar with such terms? They are common in the church today. Do you realize that this very terminology regarding our relationship as sons and daughters of God reveals our "down upon" mentality? Jesus did not view His relationship with the Father in a vertical fashion. To Him, being a Son was a horizontal relationship.

In fact, Jesus never came to give you a vertical relationship with God! He came to give you the same horizontal Father-Son relationship with God that He walked in and enjoyed. Instead of experiencing such fellowship, the majority of Christians spend their lives under this religious "down upon" relationship with God. As long as you keep such a view, you will always see Him as an angry God. It will seem to you that He is constantly down upon you and always on your case. You will believe that God brings up and points out your failures all the time. The sad thing about it is that nothing could be further from the truth. You are accepted in the beloved! *"To the praise of the glory of his grace, wherein he hath made us accepted in the beloved."* (Ephesians 1:6)

A Servant of God?

Let me put it to you this way: Have you ever spent some time with a person who is always pointing out your mistakes? Did you enjoy being with them for very long? Probably not. Are you eager to have a relationship with somebody like that? I doubt it.

May I reveal something to you? If you see God in that way, it is no wonder you do not want to spend very much time with Him! I know because my prayer life went right out the window when I started hanging around religious people. When I first got saved, I enjoyed an intimate relationship with my Abba-Father. However, over time I believed the religious people who told me differently. I felt that these "experienced" Christians knew better than naïve and inexperienced me. Religion will come in any way it can!

As Christians, we often piously declare, "I am a servant of God." As long as you view yourself as a servant, you are in trouble. In Matthew 20, the disciples were having a quibble amongst themselves regarding who would be the greatest in the Kingdom. They wanted to know who would sit at His right and left hand. In essence, they wanted to find out who would get to lord it over everybody else. Jesus spoke to them in verses 25-28 saying, *"Ye know that the princes of the Gentiles exercise dominion over them, and they that are great exercise authority upon them. But it shall not be so among you: but whosoever will be great among you, let him be your minister; and whosoever will be chief among you, let him be your servant: even as the Son of man came not to be ministered unto, but to minister, and to give his life a ransom for many."*

Who is the greatest person in the Body of Christ? Jesus! He is a Servant of all. Look at that scripture again. He encourages us to serve one another, but He does not tell us to be "servants of God." God called you to be His child—a son or daughter. Jesus, the Son of man, did not come to be ministered unto. There really is nothing you have that God wants. There is nothing you can do for God that He cannot already do for Himself. Why then does He want us? He loves us!

Mature Children Imitate

Jesus said, " I did not come for you to serve Me!" Often when we say that we are a "servant of God," we really mean that we desire to be an instrument in God's hands to bless and minister to someone else. What I am challenging here is the religious concept in our minds that causes us to view ourselves in our relationship with Him only as servants with God on His throne demanding obedience and ordering us around. Such "obedience" usually says, "I really do not want to do this, but I will because You said so." Sons are imitators - they are not just merely obedient! A true son is an imitator of his father. Mature sons do not choose to do a thing just because they want to be obedient. They do it because they know who they are.

Jesus stated, "I came to serve, not to be served." Christ did not come into your life for you to become his personal slave in the "Kingdom". Jesus came into your life to help you, not the other way around. He has something to give you. You do not have anything of your own that you can give to Him that He needs. He has something to add to your life. You do not have anything to add to His life. He is already complete and you are made complete in Him. He has come into your life to show you how to be a son. This is His divine purpose! Now that does not mean that Jesus is our errand boy, awaiting our bidding. He is our Lord and savior who came into our lives to help us live the Christ life.

Thirteen

Equal To His Father

Revolutionary Relationship

A s we have now very clearly seen, Jesus saw God as His Father. Christ's relationship with God was so very different from anything anyone had ever seen, or even conceived of, up until that time. The funny thing about it was that Jesus went to the same synagogues, read the same scriptures, and sat under pretty much the same teaching that all the other religious leaders of His day were readily familiar with. Somehow Jesus came away from all of that with a radical view of God as His Father. This view represented nothing short of a revolution for the religious mindset of His day!

139

Nobody spoke of God in this way. "God is our Father?" The very notion seemed utterly improbable and arrogantly sacrilegious to the Jewish way of thinking and relating to their God. To the Gentile mind, this seemed even more impossible! "How could "God" be our "Father"? Until Jesus started preaching, teaching, and revealing God in this manner, the religious world had never heard of such a thing. Nobody had ever spoken of Almighty God in this way!

This Father-Son relationship set Jesus apart from all the other religious leaders and teachers of His day. I used to think that He was different only because He was God in the flesh. Yet the Bible teaches us that when Jesus walked on the earth, He did not function as God in the flesh. He functioned as a human being in every way! As God incarnate, Jesus came as a baby in a manger. When He was first born, He had no idea who He was. Jesus was born a human being just like you and me!

Have you ever considered the fact that Jesus actually dirtied His diapers as an infant? Yes, He had to be potty-trained just like the rest of us! We do not normally think of Him in this way. We imagine that this baby who was God in the flesh looked up from His gloriously glowing manger thinking, "What are these idiots doing?" No! It was not so! Jesus did not immediately know these kinds of things. While growing up as a boy, He had to learn everything just like you and I had to. In Luke 2:52 it clearly tells us that Jesus had to grow and learn just like you and I have to grow and learn. *"And Jesus grew in wisdom and stature, and in favour with God and men."* (NIV) just like you and I had to."

Yet, Jesus grew up into experiencing such a relationship with His Father God that it caused Him to be separated from all the rest of the people on the earth. Knowing God intimately as His Father made His teaching and preaching ministry different from all the others. Experiencing His Father caused His attitude to stand out. This reality in Christ's life totally affected the way He responded to the people and circumstances around Him. Jesus actually believed that He was the Son of God!

"And the word was made flesh ,and dwelt among us, (and we beheld his glory, the glory as of the only begotten of the Father,) full of grace and truth." (John 1:14)

John says we beheld or saw His glory as of the only begotten of the Father. What he is saying here is that they saw Jesus and what they saw was a man. A man who believed that He was the Son of God and therefore talked, walked and carried Himself as the Son of God. He acted like the Son of God. Jesus did not try to be the Son of God. He knew and believed that He was and therefore acted accordingly.

Taught of the Lord

"O thou afflicted, tossed with tempest, and not comforted, behold, I will lay thy stones with fair colours, and lay thy foundations with sapphires. And I will make thy windows of agates, and thy gates of carbuncles, and all thy borders of pleasant stones" (Isaiah 54:11-12).

What is God talking about here? Have you ever heard of a carbuncle or an agate? They are precious stones. The Lord was saying, "I am the One who is going to adorn you in that which is most precious!"

Verse 13 continues, *"And all thy children shall be taught of the Lord; and great shall be the peace of thy children."*

The Word of God promises, "If you are taught of the Lord, if you know who God is, great shall be your peace." This is what the world is seeking—peace! Just give me peace. Just give me rest. Just give me meaning and purpose in life! The Word of God teaches us, "If you will know the Lord, if you will know God and be taught of Him, know who He really is through a right relationship with Him; great shall be your peace!"

"In righteousness shalt thou be established: thou shalt be far from oppression; for thou shalt not fear: and from terror; for it shall not come near thee" (Isaiah 54:14).

Why will you have peace? Once you get to know God for who He is, you will have great peace in your life because you will be established in righteousness. You might not really realize what I am referring to just yet, but God has provided this for all of His children. You and I are His children. We are taught of the Lord and established in His righteousness. Great is our peace!

I can see a generation of God's children who right now are being raised up of whom all this is true. Great is their peace. Their deep, abiding, and constant heart peace is what the world will readily notice. As international circumstances get worse, these believers will really stand out. The people of the world will inquire of them, "What is it with you?"

Absence Of Fear

The Word says that these ones will be far from oppression because of a lack of fear in their lives. *"Behold, they shall surely gather together, but not by me: whosoever shall gather together against thee shall fall for thy sake"* (Isaiah 54:15). Who or what shall gather? Oppression, fear, and terror shall surely gather in the world. This stuff happens in the world. The Word reveals that these things will come, but the Word of God says "...but not by Me." God did not and does not send such things, but He has promised protection nonetheless: "...whosoever shall gather together against thee shall fall for thy sake."

"Behold, I have created the smith that bloweth the coals in the fire, and that bringeth forth an instrument for his work; and I have created the waster to destroy. No weapon that is formed against thee shall prosper; and every tongue that shall rise against thee in judgment thou shalt condemn. This is the heritage of the servants of the LORD, "and their righteousness is of Me", saith the LORD" (Isaiah 54:16-17).

I always used to skip over verse 16 in order to get to verse 17 because I did not really understand its meaning. God said, "Listen, if you know who I am, there will be peace in your life because you will be established in righteousness. All these bad things will happen, but not from Me. I created the waster to destroy. I created the devil and all of his demonic forces. I was the One who originally made them, before they chose to rebel against Me. Therefore, I happen to know that he is nothing but a zero compared to you." The day will come when God will shine His light upon the one who held the world captive through fear and we will remark incredulously, "Is that really him? You have got to be kidding!"

Somehow, the church has submitted to this wrong idea that God and the devil are equally matched. We tend to think that the Kingdom of light is just barely, if that, edging out the kingdom of darkness in the fight. No, No, No my friend! God is way more powerful than the devil. He made him. He should know! No weapon formed against you shall prosper. Every tongue that rises up against you in judgment you shall condemn!

What is the power of the devil and sin in your life? The Old Covenant Law! 1 Cor 15:56 "and the power of sin is the law." When you choose to continue living under the Law, he has the power to condemn you. How has the devil's authority been destroyed?

When you were dead in your sins and in the uncircumcision of your sinful nature, God made you alive with Christ. He forgave us all our sins, having canceled the written code, with its regulations, that was against us and that stood opposed to us; he took it away, nailing it to the cross. And having disarmed the powers and authorities, he made a public spectacle of them, triumphing over them by the cross. (Colossians 2:13-15) NIV

Jesus fulfilled all the righteous requirements of the Law in your place. The righteousness that was His now became yours by faith in His name. Because you are now in Him, as far as God the Father is concerned the Law is not a valid part of your life anymore. Therefore, the devil really has nothing to accuse you of. Hallelujah! He has absolutely no rightful power in your life! Now that is good news!

"This is the heritage of the servants of the LORD, and their righteousness is of me, saith the LORD" (Isaiah 54:17). Knowing God brings you into a right relationship with Him. Jesus understood this. *"...their righteousness is of Me!"*

Jesus had a relationship with God that He was 100% sure, absolutely convinced, and totally persuaded in His heart that no matter what evil was happening to Him, it was not God doing it to Him. You and I can face anything in life if we are totally persuaded and absolutely convinced in our hearts that God is on our side. *"If God be for us, who can be against us?"* (Romans 8:31).

Religion Persecutes The Son

In John 5, Jesus healed a lame man on the Sabbath, telling him to "...take up your bed and walk." Under the Law, you were not supposed to carry anything on the Sabbath day. Picking up the story around verse 10, the man ran into some Jews who asked him, "Who healed you?" He answered, "I do not know." Then Jesus finds him again, this time in the temple. The healed fellow recognizes the Lord and tells the Jews, "It was Jesus who made me whole!" *For this reason the Jews began to persecute (annoy, torment) Jesus and sought to kill Him, because He was doing these things on the Sabbath.* Verse 16 (AMP)

These religious people annoyed and tormented Jesus. These religious folks even sought to kill him! Why?

"But Jesus answered them, My Father has worked [even] until now, [He has never ceased working; He is still working] and I, too, must be at [divine] work" (John 5:17) AMP

They asked, "What gives you the right to do these things on the Sabbath Day?"

Jesus answered, "My Father has not stopped working. He is working right now." Friend, God has not stopped working in your life! Right now, He is busy working. He has not stopped. It may not appear like it right now, but God is working.

Jesus continued, "He is still working. I too must be at divine work." Verse 18 (AMP) resumes, *"This made the Jews more determined than ever to kill Him [to do away with Him]; because He not only was breaking (weakening, violating) the Sabbath, but He actually was speaking of God as being [in a special sense] His own Father, making Himself equal [putting Himself on a level] with God."*

Why did they want to kill Jesus? Was it because He healed a man? That was what I had always thought before. I believed that they wanted to kill Jesus because He had healed a man on the Sabbath. From this scripture though, we can see clearly that even though the Sabbath violation very much irritated them, it was not the main reason for their sudden death wish upon Jesus. This murderous desire inflamed the moment they heard Him speak of God as His "Father." His professed relationship to God was the true source of their rage and anger. Why? Because they could not perceive how a human being could have a Father-Son relationship with Almighty God. The moment Jesus said, "My Father," they instantly went blind with rage and crazy with fury to the point of wanting to see Him dead. Jesus actually spoke of God as being, in a special sense, His own Father, making Himself equal with God.

The Same Today

Are you getting this? Without this revelation, your Christian life will be miserable. Mine was before I could see Him as Father. In the minds of those religious Jews, when Jesus claimed a Father-Son relationship, it meant that He was making Himself equal to God. As soon as Jesus spoke the words, "My Father" claiming this relationship with God, they knew He was saying, "My Father and I do not have this over-under, down-upon relationship". They understood that He was talking about a horizontal relationship on equal footing and not a vertical relationship of a God down upon. That made the religious people fighting mad.

You might say, "Well, that is alright for Jesus because He really is the Son of God." Friend, Jesus Christ was our prototype. We, too, are sons and daughters of God. Jesus had to believe this, just like we do. He really and actually believed this! By saying, "My Father," Jesus declared to all listening, "I am equal to and loved by My Father." Is it making you mad right now to think that anybody could say such a thing? Does it make you angry to think of a Christian saying "Abba-Father?" This is a good time to check your heart!

Fourteen

As He Is

J esus did not have an identity crisis. He saw Himself as the Son of God and God as His Father. John 1:14 (AMP) relates, *"And the Word (Christ) became flesh (human, incarnate) and tabernacled (fixed His tent of flesh, lived awhile) among us; and we [actually] saw His glory (His honor, His majesty), such glory as an only begotten son receives from his father, full of grace (favor, loving-kindness) and truth."*

Jesus walked among His disciples for several years. John, the writer of the above scripture, was one of His closest buddies. In fact, you could present a strong case for John being the closest. Closer than anybody else on earth. John wrote, "When I looked upon

149

Jesus, I saw in Him the glory of the only begotten Son of God."

John saw Jesus daily as he lived and traveled with Him. He personally observed how Jesus talked with people. He saw what Jesus thought of Himself. He was there when Jesus looked at the fig tree and cursed it by declaring, "You will never bear fruit again!" John watched Jesus take the leper by the hand and heal him. He was there when the lame man got restored. John saw Jesus raise Lazarus from the grave. He was present the whole time and said, "We beheld Jesus. We looked upon Him with our own eyes. We saw Him as the only begotten of the Father—full of grace and truth."

When Jesus walked the earth, He actually believed that He was the Son of God. Therefore, He spoke like the Son of God and acted like the Son of God. Everyone who looked upon Jesus was taken aback. They asked, "Who is this guy? Isn't His sister married to my friend? Who is this guy that He actually talks like He is the Son of God? He actually believes this about Himself!"

As you begin to believe these truths for yourself, you will start walking and talking like the Son of God. The things God promised you in the Bible will manifest. Then others will ask, "Who are you? Aren't you the one who worked with me in the factory (office, school, etc.)? I can remember you being happy all the time, but who are you?" That is Jesus in you. They beheld His glory as of the only begotten of the Father. Jesus was fully persuaded that He was the Son of God. He was fully convinced in His heart. The question is "Are you?"

One With The Father

You still might be saying in your heart, "Yeah, that was Jesus. He could do that." Stay with me as we go to John 10:30 (AMP) where Jesus boldly and clearly says, *"I and the Father are One."* Once again, Jesus was talking to the religious leaders. Can you imagine just how hard these guys must have swallowed when they heard Him say that? I imagine several of them stepped back and looked up for sudden flashes of lightning!

When none came, they took matters into their own hands. *"Again the Jews brought up stones to stone Him. Jesus said to them, My Father..."* Here Jesus is claiming a Father-Son relationship with God again. *"...My Father has enabled Me to do many good deeds. [I have shown many acts of mercy in your presence.] For which of these do you mean to stone Me? The Jews replied, We are not going to stone You for a good act, but for blasphemy, because You, a mere Man, make Yourself [out to be] God"* (John 10:31-33)AMP To them, Jesus blasphemed not by doing good works but by setting Himself on the same level as Almighty God. People are never upset when you do good works. That is not what bothers them.

When the Lord started dealing with me strongly concerning this message of grace and peace, I can remember sharing my initial concerns with my wife. There were times when I would say to her, "I cannot say what I want to say, I can't say what is in my heart, because I feel like it is blasphemy!" Really! When Jesus revealed to me these truths of grace, peace, righteousness, and understanding my relationship with Him, I would lament saying, "I cannot preach that because people will just not understand! I feel like it is blasphemy, so I cannot say it." Blasphemy rang in their religious ears every time Jesus spoke the words, "My Father."

"You, a mere Man, make yourself out to be God!" By the fact that Jesus had called God His Father, they pronounced judgment upon Him for blasphemy. Guess what? Religion has steered away from the concept of God being your Father ever since.

God-Beings

In response to their accusation, *Jesus answered them, "Is it not written in your Law, "I said", You are gods?"* [Psalm 82:6] (John 10:34) AMP

You may be thinking, "Arthur, please do not say that you are God!" No! I am not saying that we are God(s). I am saying that we as believers need to understand that when you are born again by the Holy Spirit through regeneration, you have become a God-being. When you fully realize that you really are "in Christ," a little light clicks on inside. However, when I first began to share this, my mouth did not want to say it out loud because I felt like God would strike me dead for doing so. Since then I have overcome my religious thinking and firmly realized that this is the reality of the Word of God. As born again people we are God-beings! Think about it: He lives in you and you live in Him. Being

152

so completely immersed in each other. Terminology such as "God-being" ought to be considered very appropriate by now in the Church!

"And we know (understand, recognize, are conscious of, by observation and by experience) and believe (adhere to and put faith in and rely on) the love God cherishes for us. God is love, and he who dwells and continues in love dwells and continues in God, and God dwells and continues in him. In this [union and communion with Him] love is brought to completion and attains perfection with us, that we may have confidence for the day of judgment [with assurance and boldness to face Him], because as He is, so are we in this world" (1 John 4:16-17)AMP,

Pay specific attention to the last phrase in this passage, "...because as He is, so are we in this world." Are you in this world? If not, then where are you from? Some super-spiritual Christians will answer this by emphasizing, "I am not of this world." That is not my question. I am asking, "Are you in this world?" Are you subject to what occurs in this world? If you happened to be in New York City visiting the Twin Towers on the morning of September 11, 2001, you would have been affected by the terrorists flying airplanes into them, Christian or not. As human beings living on planet earth, you and I are definitely IN this world!

The scripture states, "As Jesus is." Note that it does not say, "As Jesus was" or even "As Jesus will be." The Word here is not talking about what He was like when He walked the earth. It is talking about how He is NOW in His current resurrected state!

How is He NOW? Jesus is seated at the right hand of God the Father. "As He is so are you in this world." It is not that we will someday be seated with Christ in the heavenlies. As He is now, so are you in this world! You and I are now in Christ who is seated at the right hand of the Father. To my natural senses it might not look like I am seated at the right hand of the Father, but that is the true spiritual reality. Born again people walk in a peculiar dual citizenship between both heaven and earth. We really are in two places at once! When Jesus walked the earth, He understood this declaring, "I am the Son of God and I am the Son of man. I am both at the same time!"

...So Are You Now!

How else does this "as He is, so are you in this world" reality affect us? Is Jesus sick right now? No! As He is, so are you. "Well, why then do I still have sickness in my body?" Maybe it is because you do not yet really believe that you are a son of God. "Why am I depressed today?" Though there may be chemical processes at work contributing to this, even they are subject to your being seated at the right hand of God. "As He is, so are you in this world!" What is already eternally true of you in the spirit realm will manifest in the natural realm when you believe.

Allow me to go after the real root of things here. Is God angry with Jesus right now? No! As He is, so are you in this world. If God is not angry with Jesus, then why do you think that He would be angry with you? The only way God could be angry with you right now is if He is angry with Jesus! Is God disappointed with Jesus today? No! Then He is not disappointed in you because as He is, so are you in this world!

Jesus saw Himself equal with and loved by the Father. This fact made religious people so mad that they wanted to kill Him. If you start to believe this about yourself, there will be some religious people in this world who will want to kill you. They may not try to murder you physically, but they will try to destroy you in whatever way they can.

What Did You See?

When God created Adam, He formed him out of the dust of the ground. The Bible account tells us that God breathed into him the breath of life. At that moment, Adam became a living soul. He was a created being outside of God.

Jesus came to reveal to us our relationship with God. I used to teach that He came to restore us back to our original relationship and position. Now I know better. Jesus came to make it a much better relationship than ever before!

While I was a Bible school student, there was a time that I struggled to sleep for about three days. In fact God was trying to show me something. So finally I yielded, "Okay, Lord. Show me." That night He gave me a dream. I saw an angel flying past the throne of God. Jesus sat there to the right of God the Father. While beholding this majestic sight, the Holy Spirit asked me, "Arthur, what do you see?"

I answered, "I see Jesus seated at the right hand of God."

"I did not ask you WHO you saw. I asked WHAT you saw."

This confused me because I knew it was Jesus Himself that I saw. As I answered the same way as before, He again reiterated His question, "Jesus is WHO. I am asking you WHAT you see."

Then it dawned on me that Jesus was a human being. Here He was, a Man, seated at the right hand of God. Jesus is the second Person of the Godhead. He is also a human being. When Jesus left this earth, He did not leave His body behind. Right now there is a human being, a man, seated at the right hand of God!

Forever A Man Enthroned

The Holy Spirit spoke to me again saying, "You know, of course, that the angels are confused about this."

"Why?" I inquired.

"They come past the throne of God and see a man seated at the right hand of God as the second Person of the Godhead. They come here and see you. You are a man. How can the second person of the Godhead be a man? It is because forever and ever through the work of Jesus Christ, you and I will be counted with the second Person of the Godhead as part of His Body".

Does that sound strange to you? I saw this vision over twenty years ago, yet never told anyone of either it or my interpretation of it until just a couple of years ago. Why did I keep it a secret for so long? I thought that they would either kill or excommunicate me! I am just now starting to realize what it was God was trying to show me back then.

Forever and ever, God made you and I a part of Himself. We are eternally counted with Jesus. He is a human being. You are a human being. He lives in you. You live in Him. Who is He? He is the second Person of the Godhead! You are not just a created being separate from God any more. You are now a being who is one with God. Jesus understood this because He said, "My Father and I are One. We are One and the same. When You see Me, you see Him."

Fifteen

Servant Or Son?

When you begin to have an intimate relationship with God, things start changing. As you understand, believe, and become convinced in your heart of the fact that you are a son everything changes. It does not really matter if your flesh suit is male or female, as His born again child you are a son of God. In Christ there is neither male nor female (Galatians 3:28). All in the Body of Christ are "sons" of God. The moment you truly believe that you are God's child things will start to change in your life.

Sons serve their Father out of a vested interest. A son who serves his Father because he has a Father-son relationship will always serve better than any slave ever will. Why? He is serving out of love, not fear. In a master-slave relationship, fear motivates obedience. There is a sense of obligation and the threat of wrath and/or punishment for disobedience. A servant is always fearful of failing to measure up to the "Master's" expectations.

Motivated By Fear or Love?

Are you fearful, scared, or just continually apprehensive about possibly (or probably) disappointing God? Yes? Then you have been viewing your relationship with God the Father as a master/slave relationship. Servants have a fear of not receiving their reward. They fear punishment should they fail a given task. Their relationship with the "Master" suffers weakness, instability and emotional distance due to the nagging fear that their relationship could be terminated at any time.

"Now a slave does not remain in a household permanently (forever); the son [of the house] does remain forever" (John 8:35) AMP

As long as a Christian allows this master-slave perspective to dominate their thinking, they will not be able to abide in a healthy relationship with God. Sons abide forever! Now that is eternal security! A slave's relationship is not permanent, but a son's relationship is. Sons live in the security of perfect love. *"There is no fear in love [dread does not exist], but full-grown (complete, perfect) love turns fear out of doors and expels every trace of terror! For fear brings with it the thought of punishment, and [so] he who is afraid has not reached the full maturity of love [is not yet grown into love's complete perfection]"* (1 John 4:18) AMP

One of the characteristics that made the ministry of Jesus so different from all the others of His day was the simple fact that Jesus had no fear. Why? He understood His Father-Son relationship. He lived securely in the midst of perfect love. Because of the intimate knowledge and regular personal experience of the Father's overflowing love, there was no place in Him for fear to dwell.

A person who has a slave's mentality always wants to work for a reward, but a person who has a son's mentality simply receives his inheritance. A servant always does something in order to gain something. A son recognizes that he has an inheritance. They do not have to do anything!

Paul made this very clear, when he explained this truth to the Christians in Rome and in Galatia,

For ye have not received the spirit of bondage again to fear; but ye have received the Spirit of adoption, whereby we cry, Abba, Father. (Romans 8:15)

And because ye are sons, God hath sent forth the Spirit of his Son into your hearts, crying, Abba, Father. (Galatians 4:6)

Servant or Son?

Here in Romans and Galatians, Paul reveals that we are adopted into the family of God. In reality, the Word says that we have the Spirit of son-ship. I believe that the Holy Spirit and Paul chose this understanding of adoption or son-ship very carefully. As an adopted son or daughter in the culture of that day, you could not be disinherited. Once you had been adopted into a family, you could not be disinherited. It was illegal. But a child who is born into a family could legally be disinherited. So Paul says yes, we have been adopted! We have the Spirit of son-ship and cannot be disinherited! Hallelujah!

Reward or Inheritance?

Let us consider the passage of scripture commonly referred to as "The Prodigal Son." (It should actually be called "The Good Father!") Normally we concentrate on the prodigal, but for now let us put our attention on the elder brother.

"Now his older son was in the field. And as he came and drew near to the house, he heard music and dancing. So he called one of the servants and asked what these things meant. And he said to him, 'Your brother has come, and because he has received him safe and sound, your father has killed the fatted calf.' "But he was angry and would not go in. Therefore his father came out and pleaded with him. So he answered and said to his father, 'Lo, these many years I have been serving you; I never transgressed your commandment at any time; and yet you never gave me a young goat, that I might make merry with my friends. But as soon as this son of yours came, who has devoured your livelihood with harlots, you killed the fatted calf for him.' "And he said to him, 'Son", the

161

father said," you are always with me, and all that I have is yours. It was right that we should make merry and be glad, for your brother was dead and is alive again, and was lost and is found.'"(Luke 15:25-32)NKJV

What did he do when he saw that his younger brother had come home and his father had the fatted calf slaughtered for a feast? They were all partying to celebrate the return of this prodigal brother who had squandered everything. The older brother got very angry and would not celebrate with the rest of the family!

He proceeded to accuse his father and said, "I have been living here with you for all of my life. Never have I disobeyed even one of your commandments!" Notice here what kind of mentality this elder brother had. Only servants are always looking for commandments to obey in order to get a reward. He says, "I have not even had one scrawny little goat!" Friend, what are you looking for in your relationship with the Father—intimacy and inheritance or commandments and rewards?

It is impossible for God to reward you with something that is already yours by inheritance. The father could not reward the older son with something that was already his. Impossible! That was the essence of what the father told the elder son. "Look around you, son' the father said! "Everything that is mine is yours! You could have taken it at any time you wanted!"

The older brother had probably been the one who had personally worked so hard fattening up that calf. Day after day, he must have daydreamed what it would be like to finally be able to feast upon that prized animal with his buddies. What belongs to you by inheritance cannot be earned as a reward!

Obedience Demanded or Imitating a Father?

In a master-slave relationship obedience is demanded. Slaves obey their "Master" because they have to under threat of punishment. Sons with a close fellowship with their Father become imitators. I once heard a man of God say, "children will not necessarily do what we tell them to, but they will do what we do." This is exactly what Paul is saying here in Ephesians 5:1-2 (AMP) *"Therefore be imitators of God [copy Him and follow His example], as well-beloved children [imitate their father]." And walk in love, [esteeming and delighting in one another] as Christ loved us and gave Himself up for us, a slain offering and sacrifice to God [for you, so that it became] a sweet fragrance"* I love the way the Message Bible puts this, *"Watch what God does, and then you do it, like children who learn proper behaviour from their parents."* True obedience is when we do what we do out of love from the heart, because we have learnt proper behaviour from our Father. Now Paul goes on to explain how we learn from God as our Father. *"Mostly what God does is love you. Keep company with Him and learn a life of love. Observe how Christ loved us."*

Paul says, observe how Christ loved us. When we observe the life of Jesus and see how He loved us through His selfless act of love on the cross, we start to see and learn the true nature of God. Because Paul goes on to say that if we will observe Jesus' love for us, we will discover something so powerful. *"His love was not cautious but extravagant."* Notice the way this is put in the Message Bible. God's love was not "cautious" but "extravagant." What a powerful way to say it. I went and had a look in the Webster's Dictionary at what the word extravagant means. I found out it means, "Exceeding the limits of reason or necessity…lacking in moderation, balance and restraint". Just think about this for a moment: God's love for us was not cautious, but His love for us was willing to exceed the limits of reason and go farther than was necessary, and lacks moderation and knows no restraint. Powerful!

But the key is in the next part of this verse, *"He didn't love in order to get something from us but to give everything of Himself to us"* [MSG]. Do you see it? Once you realize that God's extravagant love was never to get something from us but to give everything He has to us, obeying Him or imitating Him becomes easy and something we want to do from the heart. God did not love so he could get something from you that He needed, He loved because you and I needed what He had to give us. I hope that you can grasp this clearly today!

Awareness of Lack or Provision?

Slaves are ever conscious of lack, but sons are always conscious of provision. Jesus feeding the multitude provides a classic example between these two contrary perspectives in Matthew 14:13-21. Verse 15 picks up the story, *"When evening came, the disciples came to Him and said, This is a remote and barren place, and the day is now over; send the throngs away into the villages to buy food for themselves."*

164

The perspective of the disciples was still that of a master-slave. "Jesus, this is a remote and barren place. There is just nothing here! Send them away to go BUY themselves some food." Lack, lack, lack!

Jesus responded to their suggestion from His Father-Son perspective challenging them saying, "They do not need to go away; YOU give them something to eat." Did the environment change? No, it was still a desolate place. Did the circumstances change? No, Jesus looked at the same situation and circumstances as the disciples. He observed the same hungry throng of people. What was the difference? He had a consciousness of provision!

Taken aback, the disciples countered, "We have nothing here but five loaves and two fish." Notice that the first thing out of their mouths was, "We have nothing!" They perceived five loaves and two fish as nothing. To their way of thinking, five loaves plus two fish equaled zero. You may be saying to yourself, "Well, yeah. It equals nothing to me too compared to their huge need!"

"He said, Bring them here to Me" (Matthew 14:18) AMP Jesus looked at those same five loaves and two fishes from the perspective of a Son, from a consciousness of provision. What did He see? More than enough!

Relationship Based on Works or Blood?

"Then He ordered the crowds to recline on the grass; and He took the five loaves and the two fish, and, looking up to heaven, He gave thanks and

blessed and broke the loaves and handed the pieces to the disciples, and the disciples gave them to the people" (Matthew 14:19) AMP

The five loaves and two fishes had not changed. The people had not changed. There were five thousand men, not to mention the women and children also present. It was a desolate place. Jesus took these five loaves and two fishes and looked up to heaven. This phrase, "looked up to heaven" has been rendered in other places *"He cast His eyes to heaven."* It has also been translated "recovering of sight." (Luke 4: 18) The circumstances were the same as what the servants saw, but Jesus recovered His sight—the way He looked at things. He remembered who He was. He remembered who His Father was.

Then what does the Word say He did? *"He gave thanks and blessed"* (Matthew 14:19) AMP. Notice that it does not say specifically that He blessed "the food," although we normally assume so. The Bible just says that He blessed. To bless is "to speak well of." I wonder who or what He spoke well of? Did Christ speak well of the food? Perhaps, but I bet He started speaking well of His Father. Jesus blessed His Father and then spoke well of Himself. "Father, You love us so much that You are not going to let these people go hungry. Thank You very much!" Jesus was conscious of His supply. We know the rest of the story. After feeding the multitude, they took up twelve baskets full of the fragments that were left over. Now that is abundance!

Works motivate and necessitate a slave's relationship to his "Master." A servant only has value for as long as they can serve.

Once they are no longer able to serve, their relationship is terminated immediately. A son's relationship to his Father is not works based, but blood based. I am a son because I was born a son. My relationship cannot be severed. It cannot be undone. It can be denied, but it cannot be severed.

Have you recognized what the devil tries to do? He will call you illegitimate and try to convince you that you are not really a son. He will try to talk you out of your inheritance. If you believe him, you can disqualify yourself (be self banished) and not experience what has already been given to you. The elder brother lived with His father, but disqualified himself from everything his father had. His father stated, "As far as I am concerned, everything is yours." However, in the son's eyes, it was not. Therefore, he could not enjoy it.

His Extended Scepter

Hebrews 1:8 (AMP) reveals, *"…the scepter of Your kingdom is a scepter of absolute righteousness…"* A scepter represents the power of the king. Esther said to Mordecai, "I do not have an audience with the king. If I go into the presence of the king uninvited, I could be killed unless he extends to me his scepter." She went in and bowed before him. She requested an audience with her husband, the king, and he extended his scepter toward her.

Esther served as a type and a shadow of the Bride of Christ. The King of kings has extended His scepter toward you. Jesus' scepter is extended toward you right now. You have been given full access to His throne of grace and much more. You have been invited and accepted. Therefore, all the promises of God are Yes and Amen.

Acknowledge Your Sonship

Have you been holding more to a master-slave relationship with God than to a Father-son relationship? Just be honest with yourself in light of what you have just read. You can see it clearly as the Holy Spirit illuminates your mind.

Many times in life we tend to think we have a certain kind of mindset, until somebody comes along and clearly marks out the territory. Only then do we see where we really are with God. This is not a bad thing! It can help us grow, if we embrace what He says to us in that time. Having just read all this, what is He revealing to you today?

Are you saying, "Arthur, I want to believe what you are sharing, but it just sounds too good to be true? Surely this cannot really be the relationship I am supposed to have with God." Friend, this is the relationship! If it sounds too good to be true, then most probably it is the Gospel!

Go Ahead And Tell Him:

Father, I come in faith. I praise and thank You that Your Word is definitely sharper than any two-edged

sword, dividing asunder the soul and the spirit, the joints and the marrow, and is the discerner of the thoughts and intents of my heart. I recognize that there are many areas where I am still not convinced in my heart that You love me, that I am Your son, and that I am accepted. Father, there are still many areas where I am still walking, talking, and acting like a slave without an inheritance.

Right now, by Your Spirit, impact my heart. Shine the light of Your Word into those very deep recesses of my thoughts. Lord, Your Word says, *"Let this mind be in you, which was also in Christ Jesus: Who being in the form of God, thought it not robbery to be equal with God"* (Philippians 2:5-6). Lord, that is where I want to be. I want to have the thoughts that Jesus had. I want to have the mind that Jesus had. I want to have the thinking that Jesus had. I thank you for this now, in the name of Jesus. Amen.

Expect God to begin changing some of the ways that you think. This means that He is going to interrupt you at times. In your near future, there will be times when you contradict God and He is not going to allow you to do that any more. Instead, He will contradict you. Be open to hear and yield to Him.

When He contradicts you, it is best to just agree (He is right anyway) admitting, "Sorry, Lord. There I go with that slave mentality again. I am looking at natural things and seeing that it equals nothing." Jesus looks at your circumstances and potential and sees more than enough. The reality of your son-ship is a mindset, a belief system, and a heart attitude. He will lead you more and more into the experience of it. Your Father is proud of you, son!

Sixteen

A Successful Life

T he Christian life is all about living easy and free from the inside out. Grace and peace are meant to dominate our hearts as we enjoy right standing before Almighty God who is our Abba-Father. Through faith in the perfect sacrifice of Jesus Christ upon the cross, we receive a brand new righteous nature. The greatest part of our eternal inheritance as sons of God is relating intimately to our beloved Father.

Even though other people would tell me that Christian living ought to be like this, personally my life of faith was strained. In fact, the longer I lived as a believer, the more strained my life became! It took me a long time to grasp the reality that the life of Christ is something that flows out of my heart. It is not some holy standard I am trying to conform to that is against my true nature. Freedom manifests as we allow the Holy Spirit to lead us into all truth. He guides us into the fulfillment of God's destiny day by day for the rest of our lives. *"For as many as are led by the Spirit of God, they are the sons of God"* (Romans 8:14). I used to think that being led by the Spirit had to be some spooky and mystical thing. Really, this verse is telling us to follow what is true in the spirit. If we will start to believe what is true in the spirit about us, we will experience our son-ship in Him.

Since understanding this, God has been able to affect great change in my life and ministry. This transformation has been the easiest thing for me, because change is not real change unless it happens effortlessly. As soon as I have to put effort into my changing, I have not really "changed." All I have done is modified my behavior. My heart remains the same. The Christian life becomes difficult when you are trying to conform to an ideal from the outside without truly changing on the inside. Conflict arises the moment we want to live holy without truly believing that we are already made holy in Christ.

Your Great Peace

Isaiah 54:11 accurately describes the conflict I used to feel, *"O thou afflicted, tossed with tempest, and not comforted..."* I felt afflicted. My heart was tossed with a tempest and not comforted. Praise God,

He did not stop there! The Lord continues, *"...behold, I will lay thy stones with fair colours, and lay thy foundations with sapphires. And I will make thy windows of agates, and thy gates of carbuncles, and all thy borders of pleasant stones"* (Isaiah 54:11-12).

God spoke through the prophet saying, "Listen, I am going to do this, not you!" I used to think that I had to be the one to do it all. I was wrong! He declared, "I am going to do this. I am going to make your life easy. I am going to adorn your life with things that are precious and beautiful." The Lord is not necessarily talking about money and material wealth here as much as He is addressing quality of life. He wants us to live a rich and valuable life in Him!

Verse 13 continues. As I have meditated on this verse, He has opened up the meaning to me more and more. *"And all thy children shall be taught of the LORD; and great shall be the peace of thy children."* I am His child. He teaches me. I walk in peace!

We tend to project this verse outside ourselves to other people instead of accepting His Word as directly to us. We often read and listen to the Word of God for somebody else. I used to! I remember reading a verse and going, "Boy, if my wife could just get a hold of this truth! She really needs to hear this and apply it to her life." At conferences I remember commenting to myself, "Oh, if my pastor could only understand this piece of wisdom. He needs it!" Then it dawned on me, God wants ME to grasp what He is saying and to apply it to MY life. I am His child. He teaches me. I walk in peace!

As His child, if you are taught of the Lord, He reveals to you who He really is. As you get to know Him better, you will find yourself in a place of intimate personal knowledge of Him. Such knowledge changes you on the inside.

External "Success"

Every human being has a built in desire to live a successful life. Success means different things to different people. To some, it may mean lots of money and things. To others, it may mean fame and recognition. As a believer, success is living a life full of wholesome, life-giving relationships with my family and friends. They benefit from my participation in their lives and I benefit from their presence in my life as we advance God's Kingdom together. This is what real success is about. Human beings were made to have these types of relationships!

Have you realized that people were not made for money? Money was created for the purpose of serving you as a tool during your brief time here on this earth. Therefore a materialistic, temporal centered view of success will only disappoint. Deep down, we all desire emotional stability. If you do not have peace, you will try to give everything you do have in order to get it.

Consider those we normally associate with "success" like movie stars, CEO's of booming businesses, and other individuals who have "made it." Fame, fortune, things, and all the "friends" money can buy are theirs to enjoy; but without real emotional stability life remains empty and unfulfilled. Apart from an intimate relationship with their Creator, true peace is out of reach for them. So what do these "successful" people do if they cannot buy or give everything away to obtain the much sought after emotional stability? They commit suicide. It has been proven over and over again.

I was reading an article about a particular actor who had experienced great success in filmmaking. He has good looks, material possessions, and fame. Yet, he cannot get off drugs because he lacks the peace that true success in life is really all about. Such is the dilemma of many high profile people that most of society will look to as "role models" in life. Whatever the external situation is, every human being yearns for the inner abundant life Jesus promised.

Seventeen

Take My Yoke

For many people today the Christian life is hard, harsh and impossible to live. I speak to people all the time who are just totally worn out and tired trying to live a good Christian life. Many are just going through the motions, they are living behind a mask. They go to church, they say the right things and they look the part. You see, in most of Christianity today we have communicated a message to people that says, "you need to live right, you need to do right, and you need to be right, but if you can't do any of that just look right. Just fake it, until you make it."

The way the church has taught the Christian life in the past, is not just hard or difficult, it is impossible! But this is not what the Word of God says about the Christian life. *"At that time Jesus began to say, I thank You, Father, Lord of heaven and earth [and I acknowledge openly and joyfully to Your honor], that You have hidden these things from the wise and clever and learned, and revealed them to babies [to the childish, untaught, and unskilled]. Yes, Father, [I praise You that] such was Your gracious will and good pleasure. All things have been entrusted and delivered to Me by My Father...,"* (Matthew 11:25-27)AMP. What "all things" did Jesus mean? The revelation of who God the Father is! Christ had been given this understanding of the Father. Therefore, we must look at Jesus closely so that we can get to know our Father and experience the Zoe-life He has provided for us.

"...and no one fully knows and accurately understands the Son except the Father..." Jesus told us, "Nobody knows the Son like the Father does." This is that word "know" that we have been looking at. It is an intimate knowledge that influences and changes the person who knows. *"...and no one fully knows and accurately understands the Father except the Son and anyone to whom the Son deliberately wills to make Him known"* (Matthew 11:27)AMP.

Under the Old Covenant, everything was done in secret. Everything was covered over. Everything had a veil. If you really wanted to know, you had to get behind the veil. Then Jesus came and did everything out in the open. When I first studied this, a little voice of doubt in my heart spoke up saying, "Yeah, but how do you know that God actually wants to make Himself known to you? Then there would be multiple reasons that would pop up in my mind trying to disqualify me from being a person to whom God would reveal Himself. "You did not read your Bible last week." "In fact, you did not attend church last week either." "You did not do this and you did not do that!" on and on it would go until I would start to agree with those thoughts.

Then one day, the Holy Spirit piped up in my heart just as loud expressing, "There is nothing more deliberate for the Father to do to reveal Himself to Arthur, than to send His own Son to come and die. Jesus was deliberately born of a virgin. He was deliberately born in a manger. He was deliberately raised in the traditions of Israel. He deliberately fulfilled His ministry. He deliberately went to the cross and died. He deliberately was raised again from the dead so that you may know the Father. More deliberate than that, you cannot get!" Now nothing is hidden from you and me. God our Father wants to be known for who He really is!

Rest

At the end of verse 27, Jesus invites us, "If you want to get to know My Father, come to Me!" *"Come to Me, all you who labor and are heavy-laden and overburdened, and I will cause you to rest [I will ease and relieve and refresh your souls]"* (Matthew 11:28 AMP). If you are one of those people laboring, heavy-laden, and overburdened, Jesus promised you rest!

Rest! Remember Moses asked, *"Lord, show me your glory and your ways so that I may know You."* God answered, *"My presence shall go with you and I will give you rest."* Rest! This is the first thing that happens when you get to know God for who He really is. Hebrews 4:9 states, *"There remaineth therefore a rest to the people of God."* You can see this more in depth by looking into Hebrews chapters 3 and 4.

Israel could not enter into the rest of God because they refused to believe that He was good. They could not believe that God wanted to be good to them. Every time something went wrong on the way out of Egypt and to the Promised Land they cried out to Moses, "Why did you bring us out of Egypt? Was it for God to kill us?" When they got to the edge of the Red Sea, they said that. When they ran out of water in the wilderness, they said that. What was in their hearts came out of their mouths. God's chosen people refused to believe that He wanted to be good to them!

This applies to you and me today! When something goes wrong in your life, do you have a thought that God has brought you to that place in order to destroy you? Do you think that God purposefully leads you to a place in order to bring hardships into your life? If you believe that, you have the same mentality as the Israelites. Therefore, you will never be able to enter into His rest either.

"And to whom sware he that they should not enter into his rest, but to them that believed not? So we see that they could not enter in because of unbelief." (Hebrews 3:18-19)

However, when you get to know God for who He really is, and you start to believe in His love, goodness and grace, the first thing He promises is, "I will give you rest."

"Take My yoke upon you and learn of Me, for I am gentle (meek) and humble (lowly) in heart, and you will find rest (relief and ease and refreshment and recreation and blessed quiet) for your souls" (Matthew 11:29) AMP. A gentle and humble person will never put pressure, manipulation and control on you. They will encourage, but not push you around by using manipulation, guilt and control.

Submission?

I have noticed that as Christians we will not tolerate the pressure of manipulation and control in any other relationship except from church leadership. We come to church and allow them to put great pressures on us to perform and to conform to their way of believing and acting. The reason we allow them to do this is because we believe God does the same. Therefore, we accept these pressures in the name of "submission." How many messages on "submission" have you heard from the pulpit lately? Whenever anybody has to put pressure on somebody else to get him or her to submit, there is an unwholesome sick relationship going on!

Wives, be subject (be submissive and adapt yourselves) to your own husbands as [a service] to the Lord. For the husband is head of the wife as Christ is the Head of the church, Himself the Savior of [His] body. As the church is subject to Christ, so let wives also be subject in everything to their husbands. Husbands, love your wives, as Christ loved the church and gave

Take my Yoke

Here in Ephesians 5 Paul tells husbands to love their wives. Wives are told to submit to their husbands. Notice that if a man will truly love his wife as Christ loved the church, not trying to get something from her but loving her in such a way that she knows that he is only wanting to give her everything he has for her. Then a wife would not have any problem submitting to the husband in everything.

It does not matter what relationship it may be, wrong pressure is out of order. Your spiritual elders should be leading you through love to a place where you love and respect them so much that receiving their counsel and submitting to them is honestly your heart's desire. But when there is pressure through guilt, fear and manipulation, it is bad news!

If you are in a church where they start putting pressure on you, may I suggest that you consider finding another church. Find a place where they are not going to put pressure on you through guilt, fear and manipulation. You may be thinking, "But Arthur, you do not preach commitment!" Commitment should not be pressurized onto people. True godly commitment comes out of the heart of someone responding to love, kindness, forgiveness, and mercy.

Come To Me!

Jesus deliberately came to make God known. *"Take My yoke upon you and learn of Me, for I am gentle (meek) and humble (lowly) in heart, and you will find rest (relief and ease and refreshment and recreation and blessed quiet) for your souls"* (Matthew 11:29) AMP. I remember when I first began to see this, I cried out, "God! That is what I need more than anything. I need rest! I want to be able to wake up in the morning and not feel like I have missed something again, thinking I might have done something wrong while sleeping." As a Christian, have you ever had a dream and woken up the next morning feeling guilty for what happened in the dream? I have.

Jesus invited us, "Come to Me and I will give you rest." Jesus is saying, "If you want to know the Father, come to Me." You may say, "But I have already accepted Jesus as my Lord and Saviour." This is a powerful evangelistic verse, but your initial entrance into salvation is not the only thing Jesus was talking about here. He said, "Come and look at Me. Come and learn of Me!"

"I will give rest to all of you who work so hard beneath a heavy yoke." That was me! And maybe that is you today. Jesus tells us to, "Wear My yoke. It fits perfectly." What does He mean? When I was a young Christian, I thought I had to be just like every minister who ever came along and inspired me to be "godly." Therefore when an evangelist ministered, I took up his yoke. Evangelists are often the kind of people who cannot understand how someone can be born again and not want to stand out on a street corner preaching to lost souls. In their minds all people must be evangelists! So when they preach they put all kinds of pressure on us to go and evangelize. So I would strive to be an evangelist. But then several months later, when a pastor ministered, I took up his yoke too. Pastors like to spend most of their time down with the sheep seeing to their feeding, rest, exercise, and wounds. Then, a prophet came by and I grabbed that yoke too! Prophets love to spend hour upon hour alone with God before emerging with a strong message for the Body. After a while, I had all of these other people's conflicting and ill-fitting yokes upon me. They were literally weighing me down!

"No! Wear the yoke Jesus gives you. It will fit you perfectly. "Let Me teach you for I am gentle and humble. You shall find rest for your soul because I give you only light burdens." People have said to me, "Oh Arthur, I have this heavy burden!" I answer, "Well, that is not from God!" The Word teaches that the "burden" He gives you is light. If God truly gave it to you, it will be light, easy, and you will be able to carry it. Usually if you have a heavy "burden," you have added somebody else's burden somewhere along the way.

Learn At Your Own Rate

"Take the burden of responsibility I give you and thereby discover your life and your destiny. I am gentle and humble. I am willing to let you learn at your own rate" (Matthew 11:29) Ben Campbell-Johnson. This was such good news to me that I started weeping when I first read it. You see I grew up as a dyslexic. In school, I was slow. Even though

I was as smart or smarter than everybody else, the fast pace threw me off.

They did not know what to do with dyslexics in those days, so they just put me in the corner. Epithets rang in my ears, "Donkey! Idiot! You are stupid!" I always felt that I was not going to get anywhere in life because I could not read and learn at the rate of everybody else. Even spiritually, I felt as though I was always lagging behind.

This scripture communicates, "If you know who God is, He will let you learn at your own rate." If it takes two thousand years, God's got the time!

"I am willing to relate to you." When you get to know God, you will find that He is willing to relate to you. "As you fellowship with Me, you will discover the meaning of your life." That is God our Father!

Worn Out

The Message Bible says it this way, *"Are you tired? Worn out? Burned out on religion? Come to me. Get away with me and you'll recover your life. I'll show you how to take a real rest."* (Matthew 11:28-29).

I like to talk to my fellow ministers, friends of mine, who have caught on to the message of God's grace and love. These pastors who have embraced the Gospel of peace usually tell me that they were not sure if they would be able to preach this. When they did, their people would begin to hang back and not be as fervent as before. As leaders they want to know.

The Lord revealed to me that He is showing people how to rest. As a pastor I used to think that nothing would happen unless I could get the people all stirred up and committing, "I am going to do it!" God says, "When you get to know Me, you will become restful. Kick your feet back!" Many church leaders cannot handle that!

When I started preaching this message, I was pastoring my first church. We had started the church and after nine years found ourselves with a building and monthly payments to make. This grace message started completely transforming my life, so I began preaching this Gospel of grace and peace. All of a sudden, every ministry in our church ceased. I was shocked! The children's ministry stopped. The youth ministry quit. Even the music ministry just kind of limped along. There I was, the pastor, sitting there thinking, "Oh God, what have I done?"

The Lord spoke to me very clearly. "Leave them alone, they are just tired. You have worn them out over these past nine years!" All the ministries had stopped. The only thing we had going was a Sunday morning service. That was it! Other ministers would ask me, "Well brother, what is God telling you? What is your vision?" I replied, "Vision? What is that?" Truthfully, I was just as worn out as the congregation was!

An awakening occurred about eighteen months later. Out of the ashes, someone came up to me and said, "I would really like to do a children's ministry." Then others began to come forward similarly. They just started springing up! It was awesome to see. People started doing things because they wanted to, not because they were doing them for me. The people began to minister because they were in love with God and were responding to His love for them!

"It is important that you know that I'm not advocating that people just do nothing for God. Not at all! It is God's purpose that we will cease from "dead works" (things we do to gain approval from God) and move into doing "good works" (things we do because we are approved and loved of God). Paul made that very clear in the book of Ephesians.

"For we are his workmanship, created in Christ Jesus unto good works, which God hath before ordained that we should walk in them" (Ephesians 2:10)

He also wrote to Titus and said, *"... these things I will that thou affirm constantly, that they which have believed in God might be careful to maintain good works. These things are good and profitable unto men"* (Titus 3:8) God wants us to do exploits for him. He wants us to impact our world with the Gospel and accomplish great things for the kingdom. As Paul says here, "these things are good and profitable for us". But God wants our good works to be as a result of who we are in Christ, instead of our good works being a result of trying to please Him or win His favour.

Unforced Rhythms Of Grace

The Message Bible continues, *"Walk with me and work with me-watch how I do it. Learn the unforced rhythms of grace. I won't lay anything heavy or ill-fitting on you. Keep company with me and you'll learn to live freely and lightly"* (Matthew 11:29-30). How did we always allow people to put these burdens on us? They were so ill-fitting! When we watch how Jesus did it, through a deep, intimate and loving relationship with his Father, we can truly start to learn the unforced rhythms of God's grace. Note: it is unforced!

"For My yoke is wholesome (useful, good—not harsh, hard, sharp, or pressing, but comfortable, gracious, and pleasant), and My burden is light and easy to be borne" (Matthew 11:30) AMP.

As you get to know God for who He really is, you will start to have fellowship with Abba-Father. That is when living the Christian life becomes light, free, and easy. It is supposed to be easy to be a believer. People used to come up to me sighing, "Pastor, the Christian life is not easy!" Having the "right" answer, I used to respond, "Well, Jesus never promised it would be easy!" Wrong! Yes, He did! I was mistaken. Even though trials and afflictions come our way, God's grace (divine ability) and peace (emotional stability) are at work in our hearts to see us through anything. Jesus invites us, "Come to Me and learn from Me. You will walk lightly, freely, and easily!" Truly we live our lives from the inside out!

Eighteen

A Friend Of Sinners

I n John 1:18 (AMP) Jesus says, *"No man has ever seen God at any time..."* You might be wondering, "How am I going to come to Jesus and get to know my Father if no man has ever seen God at any time." Lets keep on reading, *"...the only unique Son, or the only begotten God, Who is in the bosom [in the intimate presence] of the Father, He has declared Him [He has revealed Him and brought Him out where He can be seen; He has interpreted Him and He has made Him known]."*

He has declared Him! Jesus is not going to show us the Father someday in the future. He already revealed Him two thousand years ago. The problem is, we have been overlooking

Him! Through Christ's life and ministry on the earth, Jesus displayed and interpreted the Father for us. Nobody has seen Him directly except the Son. But the Son has made Him known to us.

I Would Die For You, Jesus!

In John 13, Jesus told His disciples *"I am leaving soon. I am on my way out of here." All of the disciples asked,* "What do you mean that you are out of here? You are the Messiah! Your rule and reign is to be established forever. Where are you going?" Peter spoke for so many of us when he asked in verse 36, "Lord, where are you going?" "You have just arrived. We have just discovered You. Where are you going now?"

"Jesus answered, You are not able to follow Me now where I am going, but you shall follow Me afterwards" (John 13:36) AMP. Jesus answered, "You cannot go where I am going."

Verse 37, *"What do you mean I cannot go where You are going?"* "Peter said to Him, Lord, why can't I follow You now? I will lay down my life for You.

Peter exemplifies so many of us. Do you know what we do? We ask, "Jesus, where are You going? I am going to go with You! I am so committed. I have never been so committed and so encouraged as I am right now. I am ready to follow you, Jesus. I am going to do this!" We think that all it takes to be a good man of God is enough commitment. Ministers preach this from the pulpit.

"All we need is more commitment in the church!" I now tell pastors frequently, "You do not need more commitment from your people. They are as committed now as you are ever going to get them. Some of them are even over-extended in their commitment. Peter did this when he offered, "I will die for you." He just over-extended himself!

A Place For You

"Jesus answered, Will you [really] lay down your life for Me? I assure you, most solemnly I tell you, before a rooster crows, you will deny Me [completely disown Me] three times" (John 13:38)AMP.

Imagine yourself in Peter's shoes. At this moment you are so motivated and committed, "Jesus, I am committed to You. I will die for You! Look, even if all of these guys forsake You, I am not going to do it" comes blurting out of your mouth. Then Jesus turns toward you and replies, "No, before the cock crows three times, you will deny Me." Basically He said, "You will fail Me, Peter." Wow, how offensive! I know how offended I would have been! "You are going to fail Me", was what Jesus was saying. Peter pleaded, "I will not fail You, Jesus. I am committed to You!" Jesus persisted, "You are going to fail Me three times before this night is over."

The conversation continued on into Chapter 14. *"Do not let your hearts be troubled (distressed, agitated). You believe in and adhere to and trust in and rely on God; believe in and adhere to and trust in and rely also on*

Me" (John 14:1)AMP. Jesus said some of the most amazing things here, "Peter, you are going to deny and fail Me. Yes, you are going to make a big mistake!" Peter did not deny Jesus unknowingly in the wee hours of the next morning. He knew exactly what he was doing and that it was wrong. Yet, what Jesus said next was not just for Peter, but I believe for the other disciples also.

Then Jesus says, *"Peter, even though you are going to fail and deny Me "*, meaning, "You might fail Me. You might change your mind about Me, but I will never change My mind about you." He clearly showed us a wonderful picture of the Father here. This is your Father! When you get to know Him, peace comes. "I know you are going to fail Me. You are going to make some mistakes. But do not let your heart be troubled."

"You believe in God, believe also in Me." "In My Father's house…" Who's house? Father's house! *"In My Father's house there are many dwelling places (homes). If it were not so, I would have told you; for I am going away to prepare a place for you"* (John 14:2) AMP.

"Even though you may fail Me, Peter. Even though you make a mistake. Even though you are going to totally disown Me, I am not going to disown you!" This is our Abba-Father! "How do you know, Arthur?" Jesus Himself said, *"I never say anything unless I hear My Father say it."* (John 8:38) Did Jesus say this? Yes! Then He must have heard His Father saying it too.

Winebibber

"And when (if) I go and make ready a place for you, I will come back again and will take you to Myself, that where I am you may be also" (John 14:3) AMP. "Even though you have failed Me. Even though you have made a mistake and botched it all up, I will come back for you!" Awesome! What a relief to know that even when I fail, God is not going to stop pursuing me with His love and goodness. I am His child!

"And [to the place] where I am going, you know the way. Thomas said to Him, Lord, we do not know where You are going, so how can we know the way? Jesus said to him, I am the Way and the Truth and the Life; no one comes to the Father except by (through) Me" (John 14:4-6) AMP. Basically, Jesus told us, "I am the Way. Nobody is introduced to the Father except by Me." Do you want to get to know the Father? Watch Jesus. He will introduce you to the Father.

"If you had known Me [had learned to recognize Me], you would also have known My Father. From now on, you know Him and have seen Him. Philip said to Him, Lord, show us the Father [cause us to see the Father—that is all we ask]; then we shall be satisfied. Jesus replied, Have I been with all of you for so long a time, and do you not recognize and know Me yet, Philip? Anyone who has seen Me has seen the Father. How can you say then, Show us the Father?" (John 14:7-9) AMP.

With my little dyslexic brain I used to read this and think, "Jesus, that's not fair! We do not even have a photograph of You." My thought patterns only went that far. "Nobody has a photo of

192

You, so now we cannot see You anymore. This means that we cannot see the Father either!" What Jesus was actually talking about went right over my head for a long time. Really, Jesus revealed, "If you will see Me in the pages of the Gospels, then you will see how God the Father deals with individuals. Watch how I treat people. See how I talk to and handle sinners. I am showing you the Father."

Jesus received criticism and accusations because he had no problem relating to the worst publicans and vilest sinners of society. In fact, he seemed to rather enjoy hanging out with them. The religious and political leaders even accused him of being a winebibber! *"Behold a gluttonous man, and a winebibber, a friend of publicans and sinners!"* (Luke 7:34).

You cannot call someone a "winebibber" if He did not drink wine. This might step on the toes of your theology, but think about it. You cannot accuse someone who never even drinks alcoholic beverages of being a drunkard. This was not "unfermented wine" either. The first time I realized this, I had to swallow hard. My religious mind screamed, "Jesus drink wine? It cannot be!"

There Is Room For Us!

Jesus was a friend of sinners! "If you have seen Me, then you have seen the Father." Let that sink in for a moment—God is a friend of sinners. Most people will respond, "What? I thought

Jesus is only a friend to those who are holy enough. You have to be born-again, Spirit-filled, holy, and sanctified." No! That is not what Jesus demonstrated. He said, "If you have seen Me, you have seen the Father." He was a friend of sinners.

Actually Jesus spent most of His time with sinners. This means that if Jesus spent most of His time with sinners, God will want to spend most of His time with sinners too. What an awesome example! There is hope for you and me. In fact, one translation comments that Jesus spent most of His time with the "lowest" of sinners. You cannot go lower than the lowest! There is room for you and me, praise God! So does that mean that sinners should just carry on as usual? No my friend, God loves you just the way you are, He loves sinners just the way they are. God loves us enough not to leave us the way we are. Any person who will allow Jesus into their lives will find He won't leave them the way He finds them.

This revelation of living lightly and freely has completely changed me. Every part of my life has been deeply and permanently impacted. When I wake up in the morning now, I know that something good is going to happen to me. You might ask, "But Arthur, is there any bad stuff that goes on in your life?" Sure there is, but guess what? I do not let that faze me anymore. I now know that God is on my side!

Nineteen

Valuable To God

M any Christians have a common belief that God is angry with the sinner. They feel justified in hating wicked and ungodly people "because in their minds God does!" The Bible can be quoted in different ways to "back" this premise up with scripture. Psalm 7:11 *"God judgeth the righteous, and God is angry with the wicked every day."* However, we need to hold this attitude up to the light of the New Testament. How did Jesus reveal God's heart toward sinners in the New Testament? Jesus was the very representation of God Himself walking the earth. What were His attitudes and actions toward people? Often we have been taught such things as "God only loves the righteous, and He hates the sinner. Is this really an accurate

195

and up to date picture of God our Father?

Safe and Sound

"For God so greatly loved and dearly prized the world that He [even] gave up His only begotten (unique) Son, so that whoever believes in (trusts in, clings to, relies on) Him shall not perish (come to destruction, be lost) but have eternal (everlasting) life. (John 3:16-17)AMP

One of the first things that we see in the New Testament, is that Jesus says *"For God so greatly loved and dearly prized the world…"* (AMP) Now please notice that He did not "say" for God so loved the righteous, or His people, or even those who would like to be holy! God so loved the "world!" The "world" here in the Greek is *"kosmos" by implication, the world (in a wide or narrow sense, including its inhabitants, literally or figuratively* (Biblesoft's New Exhaustive Strong's Concordance with Expanded Greek-Hebrew Dictionary.) This word is speaking about every person, saint and sinner. In fact until Jesus came and died on the cross for our sins, there were none righteous. Romans 3:9-11 *"for we have before proved both Jews and Gentiles, that they are all under sin; As it is written, There is none righteous, no, not one: There is none that understandeth, there is none that seeketh after God".* KJV

The New Testament, is all about the love of a Father for His children, and that He was willing to do whatever it would take to secure their eternal position with Him. I love the way that John 3 and verse 17 is translated in the Amplified Bible. *" For God did not send the Son into the world in order to judge (to reject, to condemn, to pass sentence on) the world, but that the world might find salvation and be made safe and sound!"* What a powerful way to say it. Def – Safe:"the provision of security and protection. Being free from the feelings of risk or danger." Def – Sound: "a state of being healthy, whole and complete. Not diseased or damaged or inferior in any way." God's whole intent is to make sure that every person has the opportunity to have his or her eternity safe and sound through Jesus Christ.

Unholy Places

The Gospels are full of what I call "Picture Perfect Moments" of Jesus in action. I want to look at just a few of these New Testament snapshots of Christ revealing His Father's heart toward sinners. Jesus painted pictures with His words and with His everyday interactions with ordinary people for us to see, understand, and follow. He is also our example as believers. Our Christian lives ought to be "stamped" with His "image" and "likeness" since we are in Him and He is in us.

[Jesus] went out again along the seashore; and all the multitude kept gathering about Him, and He kept teaching them. And as He was passing by, He saw Levi (Matthew) son of Alphaeus sitting at the tax office, and He said to him, Follow Me! [Be joined to Me as a disciple, side with My party!] And he arose and joined Him as His disciple and sided with His party and accompanied Him. And as Jesus, together with His disciples, sat at table in his [Levi's] house, many tax collectors and persons [definitely stained] with sin were dining with Him, for there were many who walked the same road

197

(followed) with Him. And the scribes [belonging to the party] of the Pharisees, when they saw that He was eating with [those definitely known to be especially wicked] sinners and tax collectors, said to His disciples, Why does He eat and drink with tax collectors and [notorious] sinners? And when Jesus heard it, He said to them, Those who are strong and well have no need of a physician, but those who are weak and sick; I came not to call the righteous ones to repentance, but sinners (the erring ones and all those not free from sin) (Mark 2:13-17) AMP

These verses spoke volumes to me as a South African. Going down to the seaside can have some very negative connotations among Christians where I live. There is said to be an undesirable atmosphere. People run around with barely a thread on. In my mind, I thought, "That is a place to stay away from. Not only are they almost naked, but the people there are also carousing fornicators who drink beer and who knows what else happens there. What a sinful, ungodly, unholy place to go!" But Jesus was not afraid to go to the beach or the seaside.

You might say, "Come on, Arthur! They did not wear thongs and bikinis in Jesus' day." Well, that is all culturally relative. Maybe they did not have all the same things we do now, but the point I want you to see is that sinners did not intimidate Jesus. What was going on in the world did not keep Him away from them. He went to where they were. Then they would turn and crowd around Him to hear what He was saying!

Imagine Jesus, the Son of God, spending a day down at the beach in Joppa. He and His disciples stroll right into the midst of all kinds of worldliness. The beach people are so in awe of Him that they follow Him. There would have been drunks standing around drinking wine and listening to Jesus as He taught. Prostitutes "dressed for success" would have been right up close and hanging on His every word.

Many believers cannot see this picture of Jesus. I have to admit that this was definitely not the mental picture I had of Him. I would have visualized this scene much differently. Jesus would have had a halo glowing behind His head. The twelve "holy ones" would have come trotting obediently down the sandy shore in rank behind Him. Like the Red Sea parting, so the sinners would have run and hidden from such manifest holiness entering their turf. Behind them, an organ would be pounding out the "Hallelujah Chorus." "Ha-llelujah! Ha-llelujah!" That is the picture religion had given me! It is the image a lot of us have of God.

Jesus declared, "If you have seen Me, you have seen the Father. I have come to reveal Him and bring Him out to where people can see who He is." Why do you think that sinners followed Him? They liked what they saw! What they heard gave them hope!

Sinful People

"And as He was passing by, He saw Levi (Matthew) son of Alphaeus sitting at the tax office..." (Mark 2:14). This was even worse! With a multitude of rabble following Him, Jesus seemed to purposefully seek out and find the lowest of the low. He spoke to a tax collector,

199

a sinner amongst sinners! Jesus did not look for the best of the bunch, but the worst of them. The Amplified Bible calls them *"...Especially wicked sinners"* (Mark 2: 16) As a religious Christian, I always used to look for the best of the sinners because at least I could still relate to them.

What did Jesus say to Levi? "If you fall down on the floor in repentance and cry out for mercy, you can follow Me!" No, Jesus did not demand that! He simply invited, "Follow Me!" Hold on, Jesus! Levi was the worst of them and all you did was say, "Follow Me?" Jesus did not even require him to change first. This is what our Father is like! When I first started comparing these things, I thought, "Now I really must be blaspheming!" As He opened my eyes, I can now see that this really is Jesus' way. He takes the worst sinners and invites them to, "Follow Him!"

"And he arose and joined Him as His disciple and sided with His party and accompanied Him. And as Jesus, together with His disciples, sat at table in his [Levi's] house..." (Mark 2:14-15) Jesus went to his house! Now you have to keep in mind that this was the worst of the worst of all the sinners. He was a money launderer. He was a man that no self-respecting Jew would have anything to do with. Let me put it to you this way: Levi was a kind of man that no self-respecting Christian in your town would have anything to do with. Do you know of any such people?

If you have been a believer for any period of time, I doubt that you still know somebody like that. Most Christians do not. We tend to isolate ourselves from unbelievers to the extent that we would not even know someone who knows anyone like that! We have become such an exclusive little bunch that we do not even touch the unbelievers anymore. Why do we do that? I believe it is because we have heard hellfire and brimstone hurled at us from sermons like, "Come out from among them. Friendship with the world is to be an enemy of God!" I know you have heard that one preached! But we have to put those things in perspective with the example that Jesus gave us of who His father is.

Think about a person you might know who is the worst kind of unbeliever that you have ever met. Imagine being invited to that person's house for a meal and a party. What do you think would take place while you were there? That is right, sin. Do you know why? Unbelievers sin! That's all they know how to do. They are good at it. In fact, most people have perfected their sins. They practice them over and over again, doing it better than before. They know all the shortcuts and how to do it to receive the very best effect.

Friendship Covenant

What is even more astonishing is what the scripture says when we read further in this passage, *"...many tax collectors and persons [definitely stained] with sin were dining with Him, for there were many who walked the same road (followed) with Him"* (Mark2:15)AMP. Jesus was outnumbered and surrounded by all of these publicans in the house of a notorious sinner. That is awesome! I love to share this because it goes so directly against our religious mental picture of

God. The scriptures are clear, there were many of "them" present.

What do you think the sinners were doing at the dinner party? They probably did not have little signs put up around the house saying, "No smoking, I am a Christian." I am sure that one of Levi's friends who always attended the parties said, "I am thirsty Levi. How about a tall cold one?" Levi, being the good host that he was, did not give his friend orange juice or a soft drink. Jack Daniels and champagne came out! They were tax collectors—rich people! They were smoking $50 cigars. I bet one of them even blew smoke rings over Jesus' head!

If you are anything like the way I used to be, you are probably getting pretty offended right about now. "Do not talk about my Jesus like that!" Christ said it Himself, "If you have seen Me, you have seen My Father!" He did not say, "No smoking or drinking in My presence. I am the Son of God." Remember—we are looking at a snapshot revealing God the Father here!

Who were the ones who got upset? *"And the scribes [belonging to the party] of the Pharisees, when they saw that He was eating with [those definitely known to be especially wicked] sinners and tax collectors, said to His disciples, Why does He eat and drink with tax collectors and [notorious] sinners?"* (Mark 2:16). Why were they so disturbed? In Jesus' day, when you sat down at a table to eat with someone, it was a universally understood cultural sign of "covenant of friendship." This meant that by seeing Him sitting down and eating with these men, their natural automatic assumption would have been "they are friends." Jesus was consciously communicating this to these notorious sinners; "I am your Friend." This is the reason why the Bible says that Jesus was called a "friend of sinners" and a "winebibber."

These religious leaders were quite offended by Jesus' actions. They must have said, "We thought He was a Rabbi. We were under the impression that He was a man of God. We considered Him to be anointed by God. Can't He see that these people are the very dregs of the world? How can He sit and eat with them?"

I Came For Them!

"And when Jesus heard it, He said to them, Those who are strong and well have no need of a physician, but those who are weak and sick; I came not to call the righteous ones to repentance, but sinners (the erring ones and all those not free from sin)" (Mark 2:17) AMP. "If you have seen Me, you have seen the Father." If Jesus hung around sinners, then God must be comfortable around sinners also. Do you know how totally contrary to our Christian thinking this is?

Please hear my heart here! I am trying to make an important observation, not criticize. We have this thing all backwards! We come to church where we have to have the atmosphere just right so that "God can arrive." We say things like, "Please do not allow that baby to cry or let that instrument be out of tune because it might "grieve the Holy Spirit." Come on, Church! Emmanuel (God with us) was comfortable being Himself in and amongst a rowdy bunch of sinners!

Those sinners were not using the best of language, but Jesus did not let that get in the way of being with them. Their profanity did not offend Him because His focus was on loving them into the Kingdom by demonstrating the Father. They needed the very eternal life Jesus came to give. How then should we follow Jesus' example?

Anointing That Attracts

Most people want to stone me when I start laying it out plain like this. I just wanted to let you know what you are getting into here. We say we want to reach the world for Jesus, but then we put up our "No smoking, I am a Christian" sign as soon as a sinner gets close. Most of us will not even let a smoker get into our cars, much less our hearts!

"Then all the tax collectors and the sinners drew near to Him to hear Him." (Luke 15:1). This is the same occasion that we have been looking at in Mark 2. Isn't this amazing? All the publicans and sinners drew near to Him to listen to what He had to say. One day as I sat reading this the Holy Spirit asked me a question. "Arthur, how many publicans and sinners are following you to hear what you have to say?"

"Oh no, God. No, no, no! I am the anointed of God. Don't You understand that I have the anointing upon me and sinners do not like to be around me?" You see, I used to pride myself on the fact that sinners used to cross over to the other side of the road when they saw me coming. I used to believe that this was a godly thing because my presence convicted them. Have you ever thought like that?

One time I walked into a café. The lady behind the counter had a cigarette in her mouth. I had just come out of a service and the anointing of God was still lingering strongly. She looked at me funny as that cigarette dangled from her mouth. I continued on my way back to the cooler to pick up a soft drink. When I came forward to pay for my beverage, this lady was still standing there looking at me funny. With a dazed, but curious, look on her face she asked, "Are you a Christian?"

"Yes, I am a Christian" came my immediate reply.

"Oh! I realized it when you walked in because I sensed something."

Do you know what happened? I became so overwhelmed with the fact that she recognized my spirituality that I missed a golden Kingdom opportunity. I could have stopped right there and endeavored to lead her to the Lord, but instead I just bought my beverage and walked out marveling at how anointed I was. "Wow! People are convicted of their sins when they come into MY presence!" I thought.

Right then, the Holy Spirit asked me, "How is it that the

Anointed One, Jesus the Messiah, attracted sinners? They did not run away. They did not pass over to the other side of the road. They actually came to Him! Could it be that the message Jesus preached is not the same as the one you are preaching?"

To be very honest with you, I was offended and did not like Him pointing that fact out to me. Do you know what I found out? The truth that can offend you the most is usually the truth that can set you free the most!

A Lost Sheep Found

"Then all the tax collectors and the sinners drew near to Him to hear Him. And the Pharisees and scribes complained, saying, "This Man receives sinners and eats with them." The religious leaders were beside themselves murmuring, "What a shame!" So He spoke this parable to them, saying: "What man of you, having a hundred sheep, if he loses one of them, does not leave the ninety-nine in the wilderness, and go after the one which is lost until he finds it? And when he has found it, he lays it on his shoulders, rejoicing. And when he comes home, he calls together his friends and neighbors, saying to them ,'Rejoice with me, for I have found my sheep which was lost!' I say to you that likewise there will be more joy in heaven over one sinner who repents than over ninety-nine just persons who need no repentance." (Luke 15:1-6) NKJV

Jesus answered them with three parables to explain why He was sitting, eating, and drinking with such sinners. Through these stories, He communicated clearly why He valued these people whom other "godly" people had so completely cast aside.

" A man has one hundred sheep and loses one" (Luke 15:4-6). I have never kept sheep myself but people who do tell me that sheep are dumb animals. Sheep easily get lost. It is just their nature to get lost. They put their head down while eating grass and move a little bit. Then they keep eating and move over a little bit more. Before too long, they are lost. That is why sheep need a shepherd. Perhaps this is why God calls us "the sheep of His pasture." We need a Good Shepherd!

So the one sheep got itself lost. The Bible tells us that the shepherd went looking for that missing animal. Notice that he left the ninety nine in the wilderness to go do it. He did not just say, "Oh well, I still have ninety-nine." Our heavenly Father does not say, "Oh well! At least I still have a couple of billion others." If someone gets lost, even though it is their nature, He is coming after them!

He announced, "I am going to go look for the one that is lost!" When he found him, he put the sheep on his shoulders and carried him home. Upon arrival, he called all his friends and said, "Let's party!" Luke 15:6 tells us that he summoned his friends and said, *"Rejoice with me, because I have found my sheep which was lost"* (AMP). Now I want you to remember that the sheep got lost because of its nature.

A Missing Coin and A Wayward Son

"Or what woman, having ten silver coins, if she loses one coin, does not light a lamp, sweep the house, and search carefully until she finds it? And when she has found it, she calls her friends and neighbors together, saying, 'Rejoice with me, for I have found the piece which I lost!' Likewise, I say to you, there is joy in the presence of the angels of God over one sinner who repents." (Luke 15:8-10) NKJV

The next story that Jesus told is about a woman, who had ten coins and lost one. She did not say, "Well, at least I still have my nine coins!" According to Jesus, she started cleaning her house, turning it upside down and inside out until she found that one missing coin. Unlike a sheep's nature, a coin cannot get itself lost. It does not jump off a table or out of a pocket and run away. A coin goes missing because of circumstances. We are not sure about this woman's circumstances and why she lost the coin, but the Bible says she searched until she found the coin and went to her friends shouting, "Rejoice with me. I found my coin! Let's have a party!"

"Then He said: *"A certain man had two sons. And the younger of them said to his father, 'Father, give me the portion of goods that falls to me.' So he divided to them his livelihood. And not many days after, the younger son gathered all together, journeyed to a far country, and there wasted his possessions with prodigal living. But when he had spent all, there arose a severe famine in that land, and he began to be in want. Then he went and joined himself to a citizen of that country, and he sent him into his fields to feed swine. And he would gladly have filled his stomach with the pods that the swine ate, and no* one gave him anything. *"But when he came to himself, he said, 'How many of my father's hired servants have bread enough and to spare, and I perish with hunger! I will arise and go to my father, and will say to him, "Father, I have sinned against heaven and before you, and I am no longer worthy to be called your son. Make me like one of your hired servants."*

"And he arose and came to his father. But when he was still a great way off, his father saw him and had compassion, and ran and fell on his neck and kissed him. And the son said to him, 'Father, I have sinned against heaven and in your sight, and am no longer worthy to be called your son.' "But the father said to his servants,' Bring out the best robe and put it on him, and put a ring on his hand and sandals on his feet. And bring the fatted calf here and kill it, and let us eat and be merry; for this my son was dead and is alive again; he was lost and is found.' And they began to be merry.

"Now his older son was in the field. And as he came and drew near to the house, he heard music and dancing. So he called one of the servants and asked what these things meant. And he said to him, 'Your brother has come, and because he has received him safe and sound, your father has killed the fatted calf.' "But he was angry and would not go in. Therefore his father came out and pleaded with him. So he answered and said to his father, 'Lo, these many years I have been serving you; I never transgressed your commandment at any time; and yet you never gave me a young goat, that I might make merry with my friends. But as soon as this son of yours came, who has devoured your livelihood with harlots, you killed the fatted calf for him.' "And he said to him, 'Son, you are always with me, and all that I have is yours. It was right that we should make merry and be glad, for your brother was dead and is alive again, and was lost and is found.'"(Luke 15:11-32) NKJV

209

Then Jesus went into the lengthier parable of the prodigal son. The son did not get lost because it was his nature neither did he get lost because of his circumstances. He wanted to get lost. He knew exactly what he was doing when he decided to get lost. When he demanded to receive his inheritance early like he did, this young man was actually saying to his father, "I cannot wait for you to die. In fact, I wish you were dead already so that I could have my inheritance." Even though he knew his choices were an insult to his father, he left because he wanted to, knowing it was wrong.

After going far from home, he spent all of his wealth in some distant city. The "friends" that the riches attracted left as soon as the money did. This young man found himself forced to find work out in the countryside where all the pig farms were. To a Jewish mind, this was just about as low as one could possibly go. We are talking intense humiliation and deep desperation here!

While feeding those swine, the wayward son came to his senses and decided to go home. He walked the whole way, stinking like a pig, perspiring, bad breath, hungry, thirsty, and rehearsing his "Let Me Be A Slave" speech. When the father saw him coming, he ran out to meet him. The father threw his arms around the lost boy and kissed him. He commanded that new clothes, shoes, and a ring be put on him. Then, it was party time as the fattened calf was slaughtered for a celebration meal!

Now Jesus gave these three parables as an answer to the scribes' and Pharisees' questions, "Why are you sitting, eating, and drinking with these wicked sinners? Why do you even give them the time of day?" Through these three stories, Jesus expressed both to the religious leaders and to the ones whom they considered to be the scum of the earth, "I do not care why these people are the way they are. I do not care if it was their nature to be this way. I do not care if it was their circumstances that caused them to be this way. In fact, I do not even care if they wanted to be this way. I love them! If they will receive Me, and if they will listen to me I will receive them and restore them to what is theirs. Let's party!" Can you see the Father? That is a snapshot of God our Father!

Let's Party!

Abba-Father declares to every wayward child, "I do not care why you are that way. Receive Me. See Me for who I really am. See Me as the One who comes to give you a robe of righteousness. See Me as the One who comes to put on you a ring of authority. See Me as the One who gives you new shoes so that your feet are shod with the Gospel of peace. You are My child. I do not see you as a mere hired hand. Let Me restore you back to your original position here in My house!" This is our Father! Hallelujah!

Let us pray! Father, thank You for Your Word that is full of pictures, snapshots, photographs of who You are and what You are actually like. I want to become even better acquainted with You.

Help me to recover my sight. Today I choose to lay

down the wrong views and opinions that I have held of You for so long. Help me to let them go. I want to see You accurately and clearly so that I can experience the Zoe-life that Your Son provided for me through His death, burial, and resurrection. I now receive by faith Your rest, peace and joy into my life. I pray that when I walk into the lives of other people, they will see You for who You really are through my life. Just like Jesus, I want to say, "If you have seen me, you have seen the Father." I believe that this is what you want for me—to be an expressed image of who You are to the lost and hurting in this world, that they may be found!

Friend, I encourage you to take some time each day to look through the Gospels at Jesus for these kinds of "Picture Perfect Moments." This will help you to restore your sight daily. Take just one story, one event, or one picture of Jesus and how He related to the people. Meditate upon it. Ask God to give you a snapshot of who He is from that portion of scripture. Let Him reveal Himself to you. As you restore your sight, all that emotional baggage that you have been carrying around will begin to fall off. Life will become easier and lighter. Enjoy His presence!

Twenty

Intimacy With Your Father

W hile reading this book, I trust the Holy Spirit has been revealing the Father to you so that you can become someone who knows and experiences Him too! You may need to go back over certain sections and read them a second, third, or even fourth time. It is very important that you grasp what has been discussed. It must penetrate and find its home in your heart. Believe me, knowing and experiencing Him is worth it! Is this a totally different representation of the Gospel than you are used to? Then you must allow your mind to be renewed. Let your heart be established in this truth. Watch your life change before your eyes.

The word "intimacy" means "having a close acquaintance or friendship with someone." It also means "experiencing a private personal knowledge, a detailed knowledge, a knowledge obtained by much study." We are going to look deeper now at having intimacy
with God.

His Goodness Leads To Repentance

In the parable of the prodigal son, we saw a beautiful picture of what the Father is really like. The prodigal came up to his dad and demanded, "Give me my inheritance! I am going to get out of here. I cannot wait until you die because I want to leave now." What a terrible insult this was! This young man knew exactly what he was doing, and yet the father granted his request. So off the lad went into the world.

He traveled to a country far away and squandered his inheritance on wild and selfish living. Notice how he could not keep his inheritance. He did not know how to work with it, wisely using and investing it. So he lost his inheritance in a relatively short amount of time. Out of money, far from home and without friends, this desperate young man sank to the lowest position possible in order just to survive the famine conditions that had descended upon that land. He took a job feeding pigs on a swine farm. No one would give him anything, so he had to eat with the pigs in order to avoid starvation. Nothing could be worse than this!

Then he remembered the goodness of his father. Have you ever noticed that the father did not send servants after his son to hunt him down and beat him up for his reckless lifestyle? His father did not restrain him from going his own path, although he probably saw the potential for destruction in his son's plans. The prodigal remembered the mercy of his father. He recalled the love of his father. His heart turned and he began to repent as he meditated on these things. It did not take too long before he decided, "Do you know what? In my father's home, the servants eat better than I am right now. They are treated better and have a place to live. I am going back!" Then he got up and left that pig farm to make his way back to his father's house. The goodness of his father turned him around!

Romans 2:4 reveals that it is the goodness of God that leads people to repentance. There is no way to preach God's wrath and anger thinking that it will motivate people to have real heartfelt change. If any behavior does change, it is motivated by fear—not love. This violates the command to love Him. People are not going to truly change from their hearts if they believe God is wrathful and angry with them. Fear can motivate you to change what you do, but only love can change your heart. The church has been preaching God's wrath and anger for two thousand years. It still has not got people to repent and turn around! Sure, we point to the handful of people who have repented and justify ourselves. But I want you to know that in these last days, we are beginning to experience a great revival. People everywhere are hearing the Gospel and are touched and repent. They are coming to their loving, forgiving Heavenly Father, but not to an angry and wrathful "Deity."

Love Feeds Intimacy

Churches were filled across the USA immediately following the widely publicized terrorist attacks that occurred on September 11, 2001. For the following two weeks or so, they were packed to capacity. Do you know what? Three weeks after this earth-shaking event, these churches were back to normal. What happened? Why did all these people suddenly show up in church and then, just as suddenly, drop back out? Let me venture to say that most of them were probably thinking, "Uh-oh! This is God's wrath, anger, and judgment raining down upon us. I had better check that my 'fire insurance' is up to date." So they quickly got themselves into these services just in case. However, the intensity of the fear did not last, so they did not stay either.

Fear will never get people to stay with God, because you cannot become intimate with someone you fear. It is impossible to develop a close, affectionate, warm relationship with a Person that you are afraid of. God wants intimacy with us. We need intimacy with Him. Love must be our heart's motivation to truly cultivate a healthy, close relationship. Intimacy comes by receiving and giving love!

"It Is Just Not Fair!"

I realize that we have already looked at this scripture in a previous chapter, but there is just so much here that it will be good to look at it again. The prodigal arrived home. The father ran out to welcome him, embracing and kissing him. The son's request to be a mere servant was denied as the father restored him to his place in the family as a son. The party really got going as the fattened calf was cooked for a celebration feast in honor of the son who had returned. However, the story did not end there.

"But his older son was in the field..." Why was he out there? He was working, of course. He was doing the right things. *"...and as he returned and came near the house, he heard music and dancing. And having called one of the servant [boys] to him, he began to ask what this meant"* (Luke 15:25-26) AMP. *"And he said to him, Your brother has come, and your father has killed that [wheat-] fattened calf, because he has received him back safe and well. But [the elder brother] was angry [with deep-seated wrath] and resolved not to go in"* (Luke 15:27-28) AMP. This older brother had stayed home after his younger brother insulted their father and left with all those goods. He had done the "right" thing. In fact, he had done everything right, but he was an angry person.

I know all about that! As a minister and as a pastor, I did all the "right" things for so many years. I was in full time ministry, but I was an angry person. The Word tells us that the older brother was angry and refused to go into the house. I can hear him yelling, "It is just not fair!"

Little Goat Or Fattened Calf?

"Then his father came out and began to plead with him, but he answered his father, Look! These many years I have served you, and I have never disobeyed your command. Yet you never gave me [so much as] a [little] kid, that I might revel and feast and be happy and make merry with my friends…" The phrase in the Greek for "little kid" means "a little, scrawny, thin, emaciated goat." *"…but when this son of yours arrived, who has devoured your estate with immoral women, you have killed for him that [wheat-]fattened calf!"* (Luke 15:28-30) AMP.

A probable factor in his being so upset was the likelihood that he had been the one diligently fattening up that calf for so long. Every time he went to feed and care for it, he entertained many different imaginations about how he would someday have such a good time partying with his friends and feasting on this special calf.

"And the father said to him, Son, you are always with me, and all that is mine is yours" (Luke 15:31) AMP. Notice how this passage of scripture has a repetitive theme of "son" throughout it. However, the particular word used here as "son" means "my dearest, beloved seed." The father was saying, "You could have had this fatted calf not because of what you do, but because you are my seed. Everything I have is yours!" Do you remember at the beginning of the story? The father gave the younger son his entire portion of the inheritance. In the eyes of the father, what was left behind was the inheritance of the older son.

It amazes me to realize how much we do without in our lives just because we do not have intimacy with our Father. I really want this point to be driven home to you. Think about it. I am awestruck to realize how much we do without in our lives just because we do not have intimacy with the Father. How much have we lost? How much have we forfeited in life only because we have never really pursued intimacy with the Father? It is a sobering thought!

The elder brother did the right thing! he stayed home with his father. He worked hard on the estate and kept his father's commandments, yet he could not enjoy his own inheritance. I can tell you because I have been there! As a believer, I was in the house and I did what was right, but I just could not enjoy the inheritance. I was just like the elder brother. Yet, a closer look at both sons reveals that neither one had real intimacy with their father up until this point in their lives. We are not told in the parable what they chose to do from that day forward, but I sure hope that they realized their father's goodness and began to cultivate close, intimate relationships with him!

Gospel of Grace

Some of us are more like the younger brother. We rebel and demand, "Give me what is rightfully mine. I am getting out of here so I can go out on my own. I do not need anybody because I can go and do it myself. Watch me!" He went his own way and what happened? He lost his inheritance. He just could not keep it.

He lacked intimacy with his father. He did not really know his own father. Sure, he knew about him. How could he not for all the years he had been raised in that house? But he did not get to know his father intimately. Because of this, he lost his inheritance.

Some of us are more like the elder brother. We stay in the house without rebelling or running away, but we still do not have or enjoy our inheritance. We run after what we think is ours, but we still want to try to earn it based upon our own merit and labor. "It is my inheritance, that I get because I am the seed, but I want to work for it! Therefore, I cannot get it." Why? God cannot give you something that is already yours by inheritance. You cannot receive your inheritance by earning it.

The Gospel of the Kingdom of God, that the New Testament reveals, is a Gospel of grace. This means that you can receive and experience your inheritance if you take it for free. However, you cannot have it if you try to pay for it. It is just that simple! Whatever you want to work for, earn, or do the right things for, you cannot have. In our lives, we often try to obtain what the Bible promises us, saying, "God, Your Word promises me this, but I cannot seem to get it. It just does not work for me!" May I tell you something that will help you? It was never supposed to "work" for you. You are supposed to take it by faith and accept it by grace.

Both sons lacked the same thing—intimacy with their Father. Without intimacy, both sons squandered their inheritance. Have you been going through your life losing everything you thought you had? Have you ever been to a place where you were really working hard, planning to get to a specific goal, yet every step forward seemed to take you two steps back? Have you been going through your life trying to get what is rightfully yours, but it always seems to be just out of your reach? Is that you today?

All I Have Is Yours!

I can remember being stuck like this. It was like I would be just at the point when I would make it, but then I would not cross over into the Promised Land. Finally, God showed me that it was my own heart sabotaging me. It was my own heart! What I believed in my heart about God my Father only allowed me to go so far before short-circuiting everything. It was not the devil. If you are having all night prayer meetings just to fight the devil, you can stop now. If things are not working it is not because the devil is your problem. You lack intimacy with your Father God.

I would get to a certain place, but then, because I lacked intimacy with my Father, my own heart would say, "You are not qualified. You cannot have this." Then I would make a stupid decision that would sabotage and undermine my whole success. I needed to know Him even more intimately. This was what I lacked.

As human beings, we want to blame everybody else. We want to blame the government, our spouses, our parents, everybody else, but the reason really comes down to a lack of intimacy with the Father. In the parable, the same thing prevented both sons from truly experiencing and enjoying their inheritance.

The perspective of the Father was, "Son, everything I have is yours! You could have had the fattened calf any time you wanted." Why did he not have it? Why could he not just go and have his party with his friends like he wanted? It was because of his beliefs concerning his father. This led him to make the decisions he made and hold the views that he held. He believed that he could not partake, so he could not. "I am feeding the stupid animal. I am fattening this thing up, but I will never be able to enjoy it. Father will never give it to me. I cannot even have a scrawny little goat!" Boy, I struggled with this thing for so many years in my Christian life.

Intimacy with God is the key to experiencing your inheritance. Intimacy with God is getting to know Him, being friends with Him. It will take some work for you to get to know God. Close relationships do not just happen. They are cultivated over time. Consider the closest earthly friendship you have right now. It may be a spouse, a sibling, a friend, or co-worker. Think about the ingredients that went into this relationship. There has been time spent together, talking and listening, as well as doing activities together.

Intimacy Is The Goal

My wife, Cathy, and I have been married for almost 29 years now. We have had over 28 years of common experiences, living together, raising kids, talking, listening, working through issues, etc. It takes work to get to know somebody!

Your purpose in working to get to know Him should be love. It will take effort and time to get to know Him well. You will be blessed in the process, but your motivation should not be solely for those blessings. God understands where you are now. You cannot help but have some mixed motives. Trust me, He will deal with those at some point along the way as you get to know Him better. Let me encourage you in this, He is the most generous and faithful Provider in the universe. A significant part of His deep love for you is expressed in meeting your needs. Yet He longs and desires for you to get to the place where you long for Him in the same way, even more than for what He can do for you. As you get to that place in your intimacy with Him, you will experience more of your inheritance by accident, just loving Him, than you ever did on purpose by pursuing Him specifically for those things. Be encouraged! This is a process. Take the next step. This is what He wants for you. His Word clearly says so.

Twenty-One

My Beloved Son

"*T*herefore do not worry and be anxious, saying, what are we going to have to eat? or, what are we going to have to drink or what are we going to have to wear? For the Gentiles (heathen) wish for and crave and diligently seek all these things, and your heavenly Father knows well that you need them all*" (Matthew 6:31-32) AMP. "Your heavenly Father, your Abba-Father, knows that you need these things!"

What is the desire of your heart if you are a father who knows that your children need these things? To provide it for them, of course! God will provide for you your daily needs, because He is your Abba-Father!

Notice what Jesus said here, *"But seek (aim at and strive after) first of all His kingdom and His righteousness (His way of doing and being right)..."* (Matthew 6:33) AMP. What is the underlying meaning of this? Intimacy! What else has Jesus said concerning the Kingdom? "The Kingdom of God is within you. Get to know God who lives in you. Find out and flow with how His Kingdom operates. Discover and move with how He likes to work. Begin to think like Him. Start to speak like Him. Act like He does. As you spend time with Him and find out these things about Him, you will find yourself walking with Him in a close and intimate relationship!

Why did Jesus say, **"...and His righteousness...?"** God is the Righteous One. That is what His name, Jehovah-tsidkenu, means—the Lord my Righteousness. His righteousness became your righteousness the moment you placed your faith in the Lord Jesus Christ. This is why you can now approach this Holy God, who is your Abba-Father, with complete confidence that you are loved and accepted before Him no matter how your day went. When you get to know God and cultivate intimacy with Him, your understanding and experience of this reality of your right standing with Him will grow stronger and stronger.

"...and then all these things taken together will be given you besides" (Matthew 6:33) AMP. What are "all these things?" Your daily needs! They will be given to you besides. Besides what? Besides your intimacy with Him. When we seek the "things" without getting to know the Father, we are going about it backwards. "Seek first the Kingdom of God." Get to know the King who is your Father. Be intimate with Him. This should be your focus, not

getting the things. Those will come besides. Your flesh will not like this because it takes trust in Him, in His character and in His Word. This gives Him pleasure!

Intimacy and Spiritual Activity

I remember talking to someone one time who updated me on how they were diligently "believing God" for something. They told me, "I prayed and I believed and I received and I am confessing the right thing without speaking anything negative."

I responded, "Well, that is wonderful and I admire what you are doing, but do you know what? I have learned that if I just concentrate on getting to know my Father, I never have to worry about my confession!"

No matter what circumstance I am facing in my life, the most important thing that remains is getting better acquainted with my wonderful Father. It does not matter what environment I am in at that moment, my focus is upon knowing Him. For many believers, their happiness depends upon their circumstances. They have to have their circumstances all in proper order before they can be happy. So they are busy praying and believing and confessing and receiving that how they want it will be how it is going to be. I understand all of those spiritual activities. Each one of them is important and has its place in a growing believer's life. However, if you get caught up in the mechanics of doing all of those things "right" in order to get what you are wanting instead of just focusing on being intimate with Him, you will get sidetracked.

If you are focused on being intimate with Him and those spiritual activities flow out of the personal relationship you have with Him, you will see all those needs met. Yet in the midst of your needs being met, the part you will enjoy the most out of the whole trial or challenging experience will be the depth of real growing intimacy you will be experiencing with Him. Praying, believing, confessing and receiving all have their place but, that place is as an outflow of your personal relationship with Him. You will never receive those things you are "believing for" without intimacy with Him. You will never get your confession right unless your focus is upon being intimate with Him. Intimacy with Father God is the master key to experiencing your inheritance!

How did Jesus come to know God as His Father? How did He develop intimacy with Him? Was it just automatically there from the beginning, or did He put forth some effort to get to know Him? Personally, I used to just assume that Christ knew. I thought that Jesus knew God intuitively. Boom—the knowledge was there! Then the Lord opened my eyes to see that the Bible tells us very clearly that this could not have been possible.

Jesus was born 100% human. As I have mentioned in the previous chapters, Jesus was just like a regular child and had to learn like all the rest of us (Luke 2:52). He learned through example, through instruction and through experiences He had, *Who, although being essentially one with God and in the form of God (possessing the fullness of the attributes which make God God), did not think this quality with God was a thing to be eagerly grasped or retained, But stripped Himself (of all privileges and rightful dignity), so as to assume the guise of a servant (slave), in that He became like men and was born a human being.*(Phil 2:6-7) AMP.

The Bible clearly states that He stripped Himself of His godly attributes and humbled Himself to become a man. Therefore, Jesus did not just intuitively know that God was His Father.

"Elohim Is Your Father"

How did He find out that God was His Father? Somebody had to tell Him. Someone had to sit Him down at some point in the early years of His life and say, "Listen, Jesus. We have a story to tell You. It is the story of how you came about." Joseph and Mary must have sat Him down as a little boy and confided, "Jesus, Joseph is not Your father." Can you imagine Jesus as a normal boy saying, "He is not My father? How can that be?" Maybe Joseph said, "So it is not all bad", "Jesus, do You know Elohim? Jehovah God?"

We know that Jesus went with His parents to the synagogue. Jewish boys were taught from a young age about Almighty God. One of the very first things that Jewish children learned was to know that God is one God. The shema says, "Hear O Israel, the Lord your God is one God."

His parents must have told Him, "Jesus! God Almighty

Elohim is Your Father." Can you imagine what Jesus must have thought as a kid hearing this? "God is my Father." If He was like my son, He would have responded, "Cool! Tell Me some more!"

I am sure that Mary must have sat down and said, "Son, let me share with you what happened. I was betrothed to Joseph, your father. I was going to be married to him soon, but we were not married yet, when angels visited and told me that You were coming. I answered, 'Yes, Lord.' Then I became pregnant with You. Angels visited Joseph too and instructed him to receive both me and You. They told him not to put me away, but that this was God's plan." How many times must Joseph and Mary have told this story to the boy they were raising in their home?

I can hear Joseph chiming in, "That's right! At the same time this was happening to your mother, the angel that woke me up told me to call you Jesus." I can just imagine Jesus as a boy asking His mother saying, "Mom, tell Me the story of the angel again!" Over and over He was told. What an impression it must have left upon Him! He learned by listening. Somebody had to tell Him. He believed what He was told. It was probably His mother. You can see in the Gospels how she always had a special love for Him.

"About My Father's Business!"

Jesus regularly went to the synagogue while growing up. The Bible tells us that by twelve years of age Jesus knew God as

His Father. He actually referred to God as His Father in the scriptures. Remember the story of how the family went to Jerusalem for the Day of Atonement? They got there, did everything required, and were a part of it. Jesus was separated somehow from His parents. Mary and Joseph started home with a caravan full of relatives and friends, assuming that Jesus was with them. Later they realized that He was absent from their company and they urgently made their way back to Jerusalem. Finally, they found Him at the temple. He had been there all along sitting and discussing things with the scribes and Pharisees.

Frantically, Mary exclaimed, "Jesus! Where have you been? How come You did not come with us?"

"Well hang on there a minute, Mom! You told Me that God is My Father, right? You said that Elohim, Almighty God, is My Father. Therefore, I am being about My Father's business!" Jesus already understood that God was His Father at twelve years of age!

The Bible tells us that He studied the scriptures. When looking through Isaiah, Ezekiel, and the Psalms, surely He pondered in His heart, "If I am the Son of Almighty God, then there must be mention of Me in His Word." So He started to study the scriptures. He found the prophecies that specify aspects of His birth. "Hey, mother was not hallucinating on some drug here when she heard that angel say that a virgin would give birth. Here is the scripture that prophesied it!"

Personally, I believe it was when Jesus was thirty years old that He received such a definite confirmation of what He already knew in His heart that He became established in this truth. He was on His way to be baptized by John the Baptist. This John happened to be His cousin and had his own angelic birth stories!

Jesus had diligently studied the scriptures. He had meditated upon and concentrated on the scriptures that spoke about His intimate relationship with the Father. If you look at any place that Jesus quoted the Old Testament, you will find that He always referred to His relationship with God and God's relationship with people. He was thirty years old and had heard these things all His life from His parents, the synagogue, and the scriptures. Now was the time to begin His ministry. He went to be baptized in water by John.

"In You I Am Well Pleased!"

At that time Jesus came from Nazareth in Galilee and was baptized by John in the Jordan. As Jesus was coming up out of the water, he saw heaven being torn open and the Spirit descending on him like a dove. And a voice came from heaven: "You are my Son, whom I love; with you I am well pleased." (Mark 1:9-11) NIV

When Jesus came up out of the water, the Spirit of God descended like a dove from heaven upon Him. Then, a voice from above announced, *"You are my Son, whom I love; with you I am well pleased."* (Mark 1:11) AMP. What an awesome experience for Jesus to have after growing up learning all those things!

For most of my Christian experience, I was taught and believed that the key to Jesus' miracle working ministry was the fact that He had been baptized in the Holy Spirit. I agree that being baptized in the Holy Spirit is an essential and important part of the supernatural Christian life but I became concerned by the fact that even after being baptized in the Holy Spirit, I was still rather weak in authority and power. I am baptized in the Holy Spirit. I speak in tongues. I had an encounter with God that was totally awesome! Yet I have come to learn that the true secret to Jesus' power was not that he was baptized in the Holy Spirit, but that His heart was established in intimacy with His Father!

Let us recap a bit. Jesus heard the stories of His birth. He studied in the synagogue and in the scriptures. To a certain degree, the truth of His Sonship had already been established in His heart. At twelve years old, He already impressed the scholars in the temple at Jerusalem and referred to Almighty God as His Father. He was baptized and the Spirit descended upon Him. Then, God the Father spoke from heaven confirming His Fatherhood and Jesus' Sonship.

You have to be aware of the fact that there were hundreds, if not thousands, of people with John the Baptist in that place. John was God's man on the scene at the time. The people had come to hear God's message through the prophet. If I were Jesus coming up out of that water and hearing that booming Voice, I would have said something like, "Hey guys! Did you all hear that? He was speaking about Me! God Almighty just told us all that I am His Son."

In fact, He not only stated "Son," but "My Beloved Son!" That word "Beloved" does not just merely mean you are the Son that I love. No! It is much stronger and more intimate than that. My wife, Cathy, is my "beloved." I love my friends and my ministry associates, but only my wife is my "beloved." I have an intimacy with her that I do not have with anyone else. I do not just love her. I am in love with her. There is a big difference! Father God declared, "You are not just My Son whom I love. You are My Son that I am in love with! When I close My eyes, I think of You. When I smell a flower, I am reminded of You. When I daydream, I dream of You."

No Desire For Sin

"I am well pleased with You!" Had Jesus ministered one message yet? No. Had Jesus cast out one demon yet? No. Had Jesus healed one person yet? No. He had not done anything yet, but God His Father told Him, "I am pleased with You. Even if You never do another thing, I am pleased with You." This was what gave Jesus the boldness to step out in the Spirit. The intimacy He had with His Father was confirmed on that day. Then, the Spirit immediately led Him into the wilderness to be tempted of the devil. He must have muttered to Himself, "The devil has no chance! Didn't you just hear? I am God's own Son. How can you tempt Me with anything, because of who I am in My Father's eyes?"

Awhile back, I received an email talking about what other Christians think about the message of God's love that we preach. They stated, "This 'love message' is just 'sloppy agape.' It is too easy on sin!" Let me tell you something! When you get to know your Father in an intimate way, it is difficult to sin. When you begin to experience His feelings toward you, it is hard to transgress. You just cannot. It is not who you are. Sin is not part of you any longer. It does not even appeal to you anymore. You will live a more holy life by accident while intimately in love with Him than you ever will by just trying to follow principles, commandments and examples!

"I am the Son of God. Can't you understand that? Devil, what you are bringing to Me does not even compare to what I already have with my Father." This kind of inner strength only comes when you have intimacy with God. I am talking about getting to know and truly experience Him. When we do not have this, we have to continually preach against sin, how to get out of sin and all the "thou shalt not's." Really, this does not help. What we preach should bring you into a closer relationship with God so that you can personally know how God feels about you.

If Jesus learned this way, how then should we learn it? In the same way! Somebody had to tell Jesus. How will you get to now? Someone must tell you! I am that someone. If I am the first person to tell you, so be it. I am writing this to communicate to you that God is your Abba-Father. Study it in the Word for yourself. Ask Him to reveal this to your heart. Be intimate with Him and be transformed!

Twenty-Two

Adopted, Accepted And Approved!

We should always study the Word of God for a purpose. For many years, I just studied the Bible for the sake of studying it. You are liable to come up with all sorts of strange doctrines when you do that. The main purpose of God's Word is not to give you a standard of morality. The heart of the New Testament is not to simply teach you right from wrong. The Word is a love letter. The purpose of the Bible is to communicate God's love. The Word does give us a standard of morality, but this is not its main purpose. The

235

Bible also teaches us right from wrong, but again that is not the main goal. The aim of the Word of God is to show you that you have a Father who loves you very much.

"Study to show thyself approved unto God, a workman that needeth not to be ashamed, rightly dividing the word of truth" (2 Timothy 2:15). For most of my Christian life, I believed this verse to mean, "Study the scriptures to prove to God that you are a workman that needs not to be ashamed." To me it meant that I must study the Word faithfully and diligently. This work of regularly studying the Bible would prove to God that I am a good student of His Word, someone who is really seeking Him. By doing this, I could demonstrate to God that I really am willing and obedient to Him. Then I would be able to rightly divide the Word of Truth. This is how many others interpret and understand this passage of scripture.

I want to walk through this verse with you now to take a closer look at what our Father wants to communicate to us today. First it says, "Study." That is the easy part. Take the Bible and dig into it. "Study to show thyself." It says that we need to show somebody. Who needs to be shown? Yourself! So you need to study in order to prove or show something to yourself. What must be shown to yourself? That you are approved of God! Study the Word of God for the purpose of finding out that you are approved, accepted and loved by God. Then you become a workman who never needs to be ashamed. Because someone who is approved, accepted and loved never has to be ashamed. Then you become a person who rightly divides the Word of Truth.

Study the Word of God to discover for yourself that you are approved, accepted and loved by your Father. If you study the Word for any other reason, you will not be able to rightly divide the Word of Truth. That is a radical statement! Before you are tempted to dismiss it, I want to encourage you to think about it for a moment. For instance, if you study the Word to find out about end-time prophecy, you will very likely come up with some of the strangest doctrines that will never balance out at the end of the day. But as you discover just as Jesus did, that you are approved, accepted and loved by your Father, He will tell you of things to come as you fellowship with Him!

Come Open-Hearted To His Word

Every time you open your Bible, your heart's intent should be, "Father, show me how much You love me. I open my heart to believe the truth about how much you accept me. Reveal to me in a deeper way what was accomplished and achieved on my behalf. Let this be firmly established in my heart." You will be amazed at what comes out of the Bible then! With this motive, I started reading scriptures that I had always read when suddenly, I saw things that I had never seen before. I was beginning to rightly divide the Word of Truth. This is the purpose for studying the Word of God.

I realize that some people will strongly disagree with me on this point. Christians have used the Word for all sorts of things. Does the Word cover many different issues? Yes, of course it does.

But what I am addressing right now is your reason for studying. The purpose of your study is to show yourself how much your Father loves you, accepts you and approves of you. Along the way, He will reveal other things to you as well. This is why He wants us to study the scriptures. If you try to use the Bible for anything other than the purpose it was created for, you will get off track.

Now that I have told you these things, you are going to have to go and study the Word of God yourself. My role has been to present some thoughts to you for the Holy Spirit to illuminate. I cannot just tell them to you, He must reveal them. Take a look at the scriptures that I have shared with you in this book. He will lead you to other passages too. Study them again so that you can become convinced in your own mind and persuaded in your heart that God is your Father who loves you, accepts you and approves of you. You are the apple of His eye. You are the object of His intense, passionate love. When He smells a beautiful fragrance, He thinks of you. He is deeply in love with you!

How shall they know these things without a preacher (Romans 10:14)? How will you know? Someone had to share these things with you. This has been my purpose in writing this book. I want to share what He has burned into my heart. He wants to show you the freedom He has revealed to me. As your brother, I want to point you to a deeper, more intimate relationship with your Heavenly Father. I do not want you to miss out on His awesome goodness!

Receive Your Father!

John 1:11-12 states, *"He came unto His own, and His own received Him not. But as many as received Him, to them gave He power to become the sons of God, even to them that believe on His name."* Will you be one of His own who receive Him? Will you live your life without ever experiencing the glorious power of being a son of God? Or will you believe and draw near to Him in intimate relationship so that you can truly experience sonship as He intended for you from the beginning? The choice is yours!

"Behold, what manner of love the Father hath bestowed upon us, that we should be called the sons of God: therefore the world knoweth us not, because it knew him not. Beloved, now are we the sons of God..." (1 John 3:1-2). Beloved! This is what God the Father called Jesus the Son when He came up out of the waters. "You are My Beloved Son!" This is how much He loves you and me too. He calls us "the sons of God." Then, He immediately calls you "beloved" just like He did with Jesus. You are the beloved of God. "Now we are the sons of God." Will it be someday in the sweet by and by when we get to heaven? No! The Word reveals, "Now we are the sons of God." We are His sons now!

"Beloved, now are we the sons of God, and it doth not yet appear what we shall be: but we know that, when He shall appear, we shall be like Him; for we shall see Him as He is" (1 John 3:2). In everyday language, Father tells us, "You are My sons now, even though at times it

might not look like it when you act differently than I would act. Even if you do not sound like Me at times when you speak to your family, friends, or to yourself, it does not change the fact that you are Mine. When you make a wrong or stupid decision, and you do not represent Me well, this does not change who you are in Me and who I am in you. I am your Father. You are My son. As You see Me for who I am more and more, you will experience Me and reflect Me in your life more and more. Then, a day will come when you will see Me completely as I am. You will look upon yourself on that day and realize that you yourself are just like Me. You are My beloved son."

"For as many as are led by the Spirit of God, they are the sons of God" (Romans 8:14). He is not telling us to be spooky in order to follow the Spirit. The Lord means that if you will just follow what is true in the Spirit, you will be led of Him. If you follow what Jesus has already done in the Spirit, you will hear the sound of God's voice saying. *"For ye have not received the spirit of bondage again to fear; but ye have received the Spirit of adoption, whereby we cry, Abba, Father"* (Romans 8:15). Jesus called upon Abba-Father in His most troubled moment. When He was reminded of His intimate relationship with His Father, the strength that rose up within Him carried Him all the way through to the Cross.

Securely Adopted

"But when the fullness of the time was come, God sent forth his Son, made of a woman, made under the law, to redeem them that were under the law,

that we might receive the adoption of sons" (Galatians 4:4-5). Adopted sons could not be disowned. Once a child was adopted, you could never disown them even though you could disown your own children. This picture speaks of the security that we have in Christ as adopted sons of Abba- Father.

"And because ye are sons, God hath sent forth the Spirit of his Son into your hearts, crying, Abba, Father. Wherefore thou art no more a servant, but a son; and if a son, then an heir of God through Christ" (Galatians 4:6-7). As a son, you are an heir of God through Christ. You are a joint-heir with Jesus. Intimacy with Father enables you to step into and enjoy your inheritance. Get to know God for who He really is. Spend time with Him. Find out how He thinks and feels about you. Let your heart be persuaded of this. Then you will find that walking in your inheritance will become something automatic. It becomes something that just happens along the way as you enjoy walking and talking with Him.

Jesus is enough! Stuff happens in this world! Things go wrong occasionally. Having this intimacy with God will carry you through. He remains enough, no matter what comes your way. Concentrate on developing an intimate relationship with God your Father through Jesus Christ His Son. "It does not matter if the world's economy goes bad and the gas prices skyrocket. It does not matter how much work is available or not. God is enough for me! Because of my relationship with Him, I will always overcome. I will always make it. It does not matter that all of my circumstances are not just right yet. My Father is more than enough for me!"

"I Set My Heart To Know You!"

The word of God instructs us to believe that we have been made righteous and to enjoy right standing with God as His sons. Then, when we are walking in this reality, the things come. We are to seek first His Kingdom and His righteousness. Then, all these necessary things will be added to you.

Father, I worship You as my King. I honor You as my Father. Thank You for all of the wonderful things that you have in store for me because you love me. Thank You for all the blessings you have deposited into my life. Thank You for everything You have planned for me. Thank You for everything that Your Son Jesus shed His precious blood to provide for me. Father, above everything else, I want to thank You for the intimate relationship with You that You have given me through your Son Jesus Christ. I am eternally grateful for how You took the initiative to reach out to me.

I set my heart to get to know You better! I purpose in my heart to come to Your Word, Your love letter to me, with the intention of allowing You to persuade and convince me of Your love, acceptance, and approval. Please open my eyes to see You for who You really are. I want to spend time fellowshipping with you. I want to experience who You are—Your mercy, Your truth, Your

grace, Your peace, Your provision, Your healing. There is nothing that You are withholding from me. There is no reason for you to do so. Jesus has done it all. Truly, in Him, all Your promises to me are "Yes" and "Amen!"

I am Your child. Your Word reveals that the moment I accepted Jesus as my Lord and Saviour, I was given power to become Your son. Father, may my understanding of what being a son means be renewed through Your Word.

This book is based on the teaching series from Arthur's library entitled "KNOWING AND EXPERIENCING GOD"

Very few people relate to God for who He really is. This is one of the biggest problems in the church today. Often Christians do not relate to God based upon New Testament truth. Many people will get to heaven and say to the Father : "You are nothing like I thought you would be." The view you have of God will directly influence the quality of life that you will live as a Christian. God will never be real to you until you have a healthy visual concept of Him as He really is. All the benefits of Christian life come out of knowing God for who He really is. Intimacy with God is the key to experiencing your inheritance.

This book, teaching, and many more teaching materials are available on CD, Mp3, and DVD in our store at
www.kingdomlifeministry.com

3801 Galileo Dr #C
Fort Collins, CO 80528
USA

Email us at info@kingdomlifeministry.com
or visit our website at www.kingdomlifeministry.com

How You Can Receive Jesus And His Holy Spirit

No matter who you are…
No matter where you are…
You matter to God!

Not because of what you do…
Nor what you've ever done…
God loves you because—God is Love!

"This is love: not that we loved God, but that He loved us and sent His Son as an atoning sacrifice for our sins" (adapted from 1 John 4:10).

"For God so loved the world that He gave His only begotten Son, that whoever believes in Him should not perish but have everlasting life" (John 3:16).

Jesus Loves You!

"As the Father loved Me, I also have loved you; abide in My love" (John 15:9).

"Greater love has no one than this, than to lay down one's life for his friends." Jesus said, "You are My friends" (John 15:13-14).

Jesus has done all the work for you!

The work is finished. Jesus did His part. All you need to do is act on it and receive it.

"If you confess with your mouth the Lord Jesus and believe in your heart that God has raised Him from the dead, you will be saved. For with the heart one believes unto righteousness, and with the mouth confession is made unto salvation" (Romans 10:9-10).

Choose God's love!

Pray this prayer from your heart…

Father, in Jesus' name, I confess with my mouth that Jesus is Lord. I believe with my heart that God raised Him from the dead. Jesus, I ask You right now to come live in me. I receive You. I confess that I'm a sinner; I receive forgiveness, and I am now a new creature in Jesus Christ.
Thank You, Jesus!

Congratulations! You are now in Christ…

A Brand New Creature

"Therefore, if anyone is in Christ, he is a new creation; old things have passed away; behold, all things have become new" (2 Corinthians 5:17).

Righteous…In Right-Standing With God

"For He made Him who knew no sin to be sin for us, that we might become the righteousness of God in Him" (2 Corinthians 5:21).

Free From Condemnation

"There is therefore now no condemnation to those who are in Christ Jesus" (Romans 8:1).

Healed—Body, Soul, And Spirit

Jesus "Himself bore our sins in His own body on the tree, that we, having died to sins, might live for righteousness—by whose stripes (wounds) you were healed" (1 Peter 2:24).

Free From Fear

"For God has not given us a spirit of fear, but of power and of love and of a sound mind" (2 Timothy 1:7).

Free From Poverty

"I have come that they may have life, and that they may have it more abundantly" (John 10:10).

Now that you are a believer in Jesus Christ, He wants to fill you with His Holy Spirit.

"…but you shall be baptized with the Holy Spirit…" (Acts 1:5).

The Holy Spirit comes to you as a gift from Jesus.

"…you shall receive the gift of the Holy Spirit" (Acts 2:38).

The Holy Spirit gives you power to live your new life.

"But you shall receive power when the Holy Spirit has come upon you" (Acts 1:8).

The Holy Spirit gives you a heavenly language.

"And they were all filled with the Holy Spirit and began to speak with other tongues, as the Spirit gave them utterance" (Acts 2:4).

Speaking in your heavenly language builds you up in your faith.

"He who speaks in a tongue edifies himself" (1 Corinthians 14:4).
"But you, beloved, building yourselves up on your most holy faith, praying in the Holy Spirit" (Jude 20).

Your mind will not understand because it is your spirit praying.

For if I pray in a tongue, my spirit prays, but my understanding is unfruitful" (1 Corinthians 14:14).

Out of your heart will flow rivers of living water.

"'He who believes in Me, as the Scripture has said, out of his heart (belly) will flow rivers of living water.' But this He spoke concerning the Holy Spirit, whom those believing in Him would receive" (John 7:38-39).

Every believer who asks for the Holy Spirit in faith, receives Him.

"How much more will your heavenly Father give the Holy Spirit to those who ask Him" (Luke 11:13)!

Let's pray right now:

Father, baptize me with Your Holy Spirit. Fill me with Your Holy Spirit. I receive Him now, in Jesus' name. Thank You, Father! Praise You, Jesus!

You have just received the Holy Spirit by faith. It is important to act on that faith by giving voice. Allow those unfamiliar syllables and words rising up out of your belly (where your spirit is) to come out of your mouth. Yield your tongue to Him by speaking aloud your new heavenly language. The Holy Spirit is giving your spirit these words in order to pray the perfect will of God for you. Isn't that awesome! You have been baptized in the Holy Spirit!

You can choose to pray in your new tongue anytime, anywhere, and as much as you want from now on for the rest of your life! The more you pray in the Spirit, the more you build yourself up in your faith supernaturally.

The power of God will help you to live your new life in Christ. He will give you the desire and ability to tell many other people what Jesus has done for you. Be bold because He is with you!

Two Tips For Getting Started In Your New Life

Read your Bible every day.

We recommend starting in the New Testament and concentrating on the Gospels at first (Matthew, Mark, Luke, and

John) because they focus most directly upon the life and teachings of Jesus Christ. If you miss a day, no need to feel condemned. Just start back up again!

Find a group of believers who love Jesus and encourage the Holy Spirit to move in their midst. Jesus wants you to grow up in your faith while being connected to other believers through meaningful relationships.

Congratulations And Welcome To God's family!

You now have millions of brothers and sisters in Christ all around the world.

If you prayed either one or both of these prayers today, please contact us so that we can rejoice with you!

Kingdom Life Ministries Intl.
Outside the USA:
PO Box 13674
Middelburg, Mpumalanga, 1050

In the USA:
3802 Galileo Dr #C
Fort Collins, CO 80528

E-mail: info@kingdomlifeministry.com
Web: www.kingdomlifeministry.com

About The Author Arthur Meintjes

Arthur has traveled the world teaching the GOOD NEWS (Gospel of Peace) and FAITH-RIGHTEOUSNESS, a message of God's unconditional love and mercy to build, repair and restore mankind. The emphasis of the message is to show people that God is kind, good and loving. He also currently serves as a lecturer at Charis Bible College in Colorado Springs, CO

The gospel is the power of God unto salvation or wholeness in every area of life. This Good News does not point out what is wrong with you. It is about what is RIGHT with you because of the finished work of the cross of Jesus Christ, in spite of what is wrong with you. Grace doesn't give permission to sin. It empowers one to live a godly life.

Arthur and his wife, Cathy established Kingdom Life Ministries in 1992. They have three grown children, Cheri, Gabby and AJ and currently reside in Colorado, USA.

Made in the USA
San Bernardino, CA
13 October 2014